**Praise for *Soul Satisfaction: Drawing Strength
from Our Biblical Mothers and Sisters*
by Elizabeth Rankin Geitz**

"Wisdom can be hard to come by for women in patriarchal organizations like churches, but Geitz gives them reason to hope....**Geitz compares her search to give women their due to a hunger, and her discoveries are a banquet.**"
Newark Star Ledger

"**Drawing on a broad spectrum of God-images and women's experience embedded in biblical tradition,** Elizabeth Geitz links these to everyday life in order to reveal the scriptural basis of our struggle for liberation and **to make us a little more conscious of the sacredness of being female.**"
Miriam Therese Winter
author of WomanWord, WomanWitness, *and* WomanWisdom

"**Geitz's gentle meditations are insightful and fresh, and her simple, direct questions could be transforming,** when considered carefully or acted upon....an excellent book for group discussions."
Wichita Eagle

W9-BIU-404

More Praise...

"As a male I am much moved by the reflections that come forth in such short but sound writings, where appropriate biblical verses relate to many of life's situations. *Soul Satisfaction* is a healthy book **full of affirmative encouragement to women and supportive understandings for men....the contents are strong, not syrupy; profound, not pious; and realistic, not romantic**. Elizabeth Geitz has written the model for future titles in this new devotional series."

Harrison T. Simons
Education/Liturgy Resources, Oxford, North Carolina

"In *Soul Satisfaction*, Elizabeth Geitz once again demonstrates her keen mind and depth of theological understanding. She is writing as a scholarly priest, but more important, she is writing as a Christian woman-daughter, wife, sister, and mother. This is a **personal, indeed intimate, work, as the author does not seek to distance herself behind abstraction, but rather engages the reader in a dialogue that is simultaneously challenging and comforting.** This book deserves to be read deliberately and prayerfully.

Margaret Guenther
author of Holy Listening *and* Toward Holy Ground

More Praise...

"In wallop-packed dollops of two to five paragraphs, [Geitz] introduces you to one scriptural passage after a bookful of others that affirm and support the strength and personhood of women. **She raises your consciousness about what the Bible really says about women while nudging your conscience toward ministering to others.**"

Sally M. Bucklee
Episcopal Women's Caucus,
Former President

Other books by Elizabeth Rankin Geitz
Gender and the Nicene Creed*
Entertaining Angels*
Welcoming the Stranger
Recovering Lost Tradition

*Published by Morehouse Publishing

Soul Satisfaction

Drawing Strength from Our Biblical Mothers and Sisters

ELIZABETH RANKIN GEITZ

MOREHOUSE PUBLISHING

Morehouse Publishing
P.O. Box 1321
Harrisburg, PA 17105

Morehouse Publishing is a division of the Morehouse Group.

Printed in the United States of America
03 02 01 00 99 98   10 9 8 7 6 5 4 3 2

Cover art: SuperStock. *Madonna and Child and Saints from Convent Sion* by Gerard David. Musee des Beaux Arts, Rouen, France. ET Archive, London.
Cover design by Trude Brummer

Geitz, Elizabeth Rankin.
        Soul satisfaction: drawing strength from our biblical mothers and sisters/Elizabeth Rankin Geitz.
            p. cm.
        Includes bibliographical references.
        ISBN 0-8192-1737-9 (pbk.)
        1. Women in the Bible—Meditations. 2. Women—Prayer-books and devotions—English. 3. Self-esteem in women—Religious aspects—Christianity—Prayer-books and devotions—English. I. Title.
BS575.G45 1998
220.9'2'082—dc21

                                                                                98-11080
                                                                                      CIP

DEDICATED

With heartfelt gratitude for the life and ministry of
The Reverend Dr. Margaret Guenther and
Sister Lorette Piper, RSCJ,
with whom I continue to experience the love
of God as Mother—what a blessing,

and

with joy and thanksgiving for the Women of
Prodigal Daughters
Sarah's Sisters
Trinity Cathedral Women's Group
Episcopal Women's Caucus
Clergy Moms and
Creative Journey Episcopal Women of New Jersey
who have discovered, shared, struggled with,
and embraced these texts with me.

Glory to God and God Alone

ACKNOWLEDGMENTS

First and most important, I would like to thank my husband, Michael, and my children, Charlotte and Michael R., with all my heart, for loving me enough to give me the time to write this book and for supporting me each step of the way. Your love makes it all worthwhile.

In addition, I would like to thank Sister Elias Freeman for the inspiration her books have given to me, and the Reverend Dr. Dee Dee Turlington for her editorial advice. Many thanks go also to my friends and family who have read the manuscript at its various stages and have shared their insights with me. My thanks to you all.

Grateful acknowledgment is made to the following publishers for permission to use the works cited:

Brentwood-Benson Music Publishing. "I Go to the Rock" words and music by Dottie Rambo (copyright 1977 John T. Benson Publishing/ASCAP).

The Crossroad Publishing Company. Prayer by Miriam Therese Winter in *WomanWord: A Feminist Lectionary and Psalter on Women of the New Testament* (copyright 1990), 237. Also published by HarperCollins in the UK/Commonwealth.

HarperCollins Publishers. Excerpt from *A Return to Love* by Marianne Williamson (copyright 1992), 165.

My soul is satisfied as with a rich feast,
and my mouth praises you with joyful lips.

Psalm 63:5

INTRODUCTION

A month before my mother took her own life, she said to me, "Elizabeth, I don't have any trouble with a patriarchal society. I like a male-dominated world." My mother's suicide occurred when I was in seminary studying to be an Episcopal priest. Now, as a mother, wife, priest, and published author, I am working through my own personal pain and grief, as well as the pastoral implications of my mother's death.

On that fateful morning in 1991, two books lay on my mother's bedside table—the Bible and *Women and Self-Esteem*. What had gone wrong? Why is it that throughout the history of the church Holy Scripture has been used against women, telling them they are second-rate, denigrating their very personhood? Could this possibly be God's will? Standing at the foot of my mother's bed that day I knew it could not be so, and I knew that I was meant to tell the world a different story.

As I began to work through my grief, the image of the two books would not leave me. Could biblical teaching about women ever be reconciled with a book on women and self-esteem? Since the institutional church has traditionally taught that woman was created second and sinned first, I wondered. Then I prayed for God to show me the way.

I began to study the feminine in Scripture, and parts of the biblical tradition I never knew existed suddenly unfolded before me. I found that there were biblical women filled with a positive sense of self who exhibited great courage and leadership. Why had I never heard of them? There was passage after passage in which Jesus upheld the very personhood of women. Not only did he consistently affirm women, but his first resurrection appearance was to a woman, Mary Magdalene. In addition, there were powerful feminine images of God. Throughout Scripture, God is imaged not only as a father, but also as a woman in labor giving birth to creation and as a comforting mother. Yes, women too are created in the image of God, and so was my mother. Unfortunately, she never knew it.

In *Women at the Well*, Kathleen Fischer writes of the "significance religious imagery has for a woman's sense of authority of the self." She continues, "Images of God and self are very closely connected, and a change in one brings about a change in the other. This is borne out by testimony from contemporary women who state that a new awareness of their own authority followed upon changes in their image of God. Rather than being an external force, God became the source of a new inner power."[1]

As women today struggle for new sources of inner power, it pains me to see so many turning to the latest self-help books, New Age religions, or passing fads.

All we need, all we have ever needed, is in the Bible. However, the good news for women in Scripture has been twisted beyond recognition, taken out of context, or simply never mentioned at all. This misuse of Holy Scripture, to keep a patriarchal power system in place, is nothing short of sin. And it is a sin we can no longer afford to ignore.

We live in a world in which adolescent girls are increasingly prey to depression, eating disorders, addictions, and suicide attempts;[2] at a minimum, twice as many women are depressed as are men;[3] women are three times more likely to attempt suicide;[4] and more than one-third of female homicide victims are killed by their husbands or boyfriends.[5]

The image that women have of themselves and that men have of women is shaped by the world in which we live, a world in which many "isms" predominate, one of which is sexism. God did not create a world in which one sex was meant to be dominant. Rather, God created a world in which women and men are meant to live as equal partners.

Soul Satisfaction: Drawing Strength from Our Biblical Mothers and Sisters is a book about mutual partnerships, rather than domination; empowerment, rather than despair; joy, rather than grief.

It is written by the grace of God for women everywhere whose souls hunger for something more. As you draw strength from these passages of Scripture, all of which affirm and support the personhood of women, may your soul be filled with satisfaction.

In Psalm 63, the psalmist rejoices, "My soul is satisfied as with a rich feast, and my mouth praises you with joyful lips." Let us praise God with all our heart and soul, as we enjoy this rich feast God has prepared for us all.

1. Kathleen Fischer, *Women at the Well* (New York: Paulist Press, 1988), 60.
2. Mary Pipher, *Reviving Ophelia: Saving the Selves of Adolescent Girls* (New York: Ballantine Books, 1994), 27.
3. Christie Cogad Neuger, "Women's Depression: Lives at Risk," in *Women in Travail and Transition: A New Pastoral Care* edited by Maxine Glaz and Jeanne Moessner (Minneapolis: Fortress Press, 1991), 147.
4. Adina Wrobleski, *Suicide: Why?* (Minneapolis: AFTERWORDS, 1989), 21.
5. Federal Bureau of Investigation, *Crime in the United States: Uniform Crime Reports* (Washington, D.C.: Government Printing Office).

*Morning by morning (God) wakens—wakens my ear to listen as those who
are taught. The LORD God has opened my ear.*
Isaiah 50:4–5

Dawn breaks and I am awakened, as daylight gradually floods through my
window. Sometimes I wake up with a sense of anticipation, wondering
what the day will bring. At other times I feel more reflective, and something
inside me yearns to write, both to sort out my feelings and to share them with
others.

When I write, I feel as if I am in dialogue. For you see, I feel as if I know you,
and, perhaps, in a way I do. Why? For some reason God has led you to read this
book, and for some reason God has led me to write it. There is within this relationship of author and reader a bond that transcends space and time. How
blessed I feel for you and for the gifts of communication God has given to me.

As you begin your journey through the pages of this book, remember, the
Lord has opened your ears to hear all the words of Scripture, especially those that
affirm your very being as a woman.

What might happen if you opened yourself to the healing grace of God's
words for you?

For in his own image God made humankind.

Genesis 9:6

Before attending seminary, I was a teacher at an inner-city Catholic settlement house in Trenton, New Jersey. One morning, one of my students, who was homeless, was particularly agitated. I took Emma into another room to talk, where used clothing was stored for resale in the community. She stood there in the midst of musty boxes piled high, in clothes she had worn for two weeks. She told me over and over that someday people would not judge her by her outward appearance, but would see her for the type of person she was and for the type of heart she had. "Emma has a good heart," she said, "if only people would see it." She just stood there patting her heart, repeating these words to me.

Each and every one of us is created in God's image—black and white, female and male, rich and poor, young and old, gay and straight. What if all people were treated as if they were made in the very image of the Divine? How might this affect the self-image of the increasing number of women living in poverty today? How might it affect yours?

Then [Moses' sister] Miriam said to Pharaoh's daughter, "Shall I go and get you a nurse from the Hebrew women to nurse the child for you?"
Exodus 2:7

At the time Moses is born, the king decrees that all male babies are to be killed. As a result, Moses' mother hides him for three months. She then places him in a papyrus basket in the river, as Moses' sister, Miriam, watches from a distance. While the king's daughter is bathing, she sees the baby and rescues him. Although only a slave girl, Miriam immediately addresses the princess and offers to find a Hebrew woman to nurse the baby. Who does this ingenious girl choose? Moses' own mother. Though only a child, Miriam saves Moses' life, forever changing the course of religious history.

There are times when our voices can change the course of events as well. Yet it's often hard to make the decision to speak out in a difficult situation. How much safer it can feel to sit back and let events unfold, rather than take a stand.

Have you ever taken a risk and spoken out when others were afraid? How did it feel? If not, what changes would you need to make to be more like Miriam?

When God created humankind, he made them in the likeness of God. Male and female he created them.

Genesis 5:1–2

My Uncle Billy Rankin has been a prankster all of his life. In high school, he was the nemesis of the school librarian. At his forty-fifth high school reunion, he walked up to the librarian with his hand outstretched and said with great gusto, "Mrs. Stanton, let's shake hands and let bygones be bygones." With her gray hair in tight curls, she pursed her lips, looked him straight in the eye, and said, "Drop dead, Rankin." Then she turned on her heel and walked off.

Forgiveness is a tricky thing. Some people can forgive a drunk driver who killed their child, while others can't forgive a schoolboy prank. Yet, at different times we are all called by God to forgive someone created in the likeness of God, as are we. Central to our ability to accept others is our ability to accept that we, too, are created in the likeness of God. For women this can be especially difficult when God is imaged only as male in the church.

What would it take for you to accept yourself as created in the image of God? Whom else do you need to see as created in God's likeness?

While they were at Hazeroth, Miriam and Aaron spoke against Moses because of the Cushite woman whom he had married.... Then the LORD came down in a pillar of cloud, and stood at the entrance of the tent, and called Aaron and Miriam; and they both came forward.... And the anger of the LORD was kindled against them, and he departed.

Numbers 12:1, 5, 9

A s a Hebrew, Moses is expected to marry a Hebrew woman, yet instead he marries outside of his own race. Moses' second wife is a Cushite, an Ethiopian, and therefore, an African. Both Miriam and Aaron, Moses' sister and brother, speak out against the marriage and are severely reprimanded by God. In fact, we are told that God's anger is kindled against them.

When the Bible was misused to support the existence of slavery during the Civil War, this passage was most certainly ignored. In fact, it has been ignored throughout the history of the church.

Today, our world is increasingly riddled with racial strife. There is a disturbing movement away from love toward bias and hatred. Yet, nothing could be further from Jesus' injunction, "You shall love your neighbor as yourself" (Matthew 22:39)—not certain neighbors who look and act like we do, but all neighbors.

Is there a message in this passage for us today? What might it be?

Thus says God, the LORD,... "I will cry out like a woman in labor, I will gasp and pant."

Isaiah 42:5, 14

W hat is your image of God?" I often ask when I lead adult education classes. Inevitably, the response is the same. "An old man with a beard, a king, a judge, a father, a shepherd," is the reply. "Any more?" I ask. "Well, I don't see God as a person, more as a spirit," some add.

"What about the image of God as a woman in labor? Have you ever heard of that?" I ask. Blank stares and giggles come my way. "It's right here in the Bible. It really is," I say, pointing to an appropriate passage of Scripture. Heads shake in disbelief.

Such images of God were not as unusual six hundred years ago as they seem to be today. The mystics were especially fond of feminine images for God. In the fourteenth century, Meister Eckhart, a medieval Christian mystic, wrote: "What does God do all day long? God gives birth. From all eternity God lies on a maternity bed giving birth."[1]

What a powerful image of God, Creator of heaven and earth. How affirming to us as women! How might this inform your image of God?

1. Quoted in Matthew Fox, *Original Blessing* (Santa Fe, N. Mex.: Bear & Company Publishing, 1983), 220.

Paul,... To all God's beloved in Rome:... We know that the whole creation has been groaning in labor pains until now; and not only the creation, but we ourselves, who have the first fruits of the Spirit, groan inwardly while we wait for adoption, the redemption of our bodies.

Romans 1:1, 7; 8:22–23

I n an interview with the BBC before her untimely death, Diana, Princess of Wales, remarked, "I think the biggest disease the world suffers from is the disease of people feeling unloved." Such a statement made by one of the most beloved and most photographed women in the world makes you stop and think. All the material possessions, fame, and glamorous holidays could not fill the void at the center of her soul that said, "There's more to life than this."

Saint Paul describes all created order as groaning in labor, awaiting the birth of God's reign on earth. Yet God's reign here cannot begin until we accept and receive the love God so freely gives to each one of us. Until we can accept, deep in our souls, that God loves us with a love that knows no limits, creation will continue to groan in labor. We must never forget that regardless of what messages we receive on earth, we are loved unconditionally by the God who gave us birth, just for being who we are.

Can you let God's love be born anew within you, this very moment?

[Rahab said to Joshua's men], "The LORD your God is indeed God in heaven above and on earth below. Now then, since I have dealt kindly with you, swear to me by the LORD that you in turn will deal kindly with my family."
                                                              Joshua 2:11–12

When Moses dies, Joshua is chosen by God to lead the Israelites into the promised land. Since they have to overtake the city of Jericho to reach their destination, Joshua sends two spies ahead to the city as scouts. They come to the home of Rahab, a prostitute, who cunningly hides them on her roof under stalks of flax. The king suspects the spies' presence and questions Rahab, who risks her life by deceiving the king and sending his men in the wrong direction. When all is safe, Rahab declares her belief in Joshua's God, then asks for mercy for her family when her city is overtaken.

Rahab's first thoughts in time of danger are not of herself, but of her family. Not only does her courage and ingenuity save her own family, but she saves all the Israelite people as well. Without Rahab they may never have reached the promised land.

Protecting our family is not always easy in today's world. Is there a situation in which you need courage to protect your family? What is it?

So God created humankind in his image, in the image of God he created them; male and female he created them…. God saw everything that he had made, and indeed, it was very good.

Genesis 1:27, 31

O ur daughter Charlotte was thirteen years old when the Anita Hill hearings were televised. As we watched the congressional leaders in action, I explained to her how the proceedings worked. I then added, "You know, Charlotte, you could be a congresswoman someday." "I could never do that, Mom," she said, with mild irritation in her voice. "They're all men." I then realized Anita Hill was facing a panel of fourteen white males in dark suits.

Such visual images communicate powerful messages. Even more powerful is the historical use of only male images to describe God, even though such exclusive imaging is not in keeping with the biblical tradition.

There are two creation accounts in Genesis; this is the first. In the great work of creation, the crowning glory is realized when male and female are created on the sixth day. Here the equality of woman and man is apparent, since both are created simultaneously in the image of God.

Think of it! Look in the mirror. You are created in God's image, and you are, indeed, very good. God has said so. Why is it so easy to believe the messages that tell us otherwise?

The twelve were with [Jesus], as well as some women who had been cured of evil spirits and infirmities:... Joanna, the wife of Herod's steward Chuza, and Susanna, and many others, who provided for them out of their resources.
Luke 8:1–3

J oanna, the wife of King Herod's minister of finance, leaves her husband to follow Jesus, a poor social revolutionary. She is the only politically connected person to do so. As a woman of wealth, she provides for the group around Jesus. Without Joanna and others like her, Jesus' ministry might have been quite different.

For a woman to leave her husband, to begin a new life on her own, was quite a scandal in Joanna's day. As such, she has been ignored by biblical scholars, becoming one of the invisible women of the Gospels.

Divorced women today can feel invisible. Suddenly, everything in their life is changed. Some experience the fact that their married friends don't include them anymore; they become a woman not to be trusted.

Women who make difficult, life-changing decisions need our support. Is there someone, like Joanna, to whom you could reach out today, easing her burden?

Then the LORD God said, "It is not good that the man should be alone; I will make him a helper as his partner"…. And the rib that the LORD God had taken from the man he made into a woman.

Genesis 2:18, 22

I n this second creation account in Genesis, woman is created out of the rib of man to be his helper. When words are translated into English from Hebrew, important shades of meaning can be lost.[1] The English word *helper* is often used to describe an assistant. However, this is not the intent of the original Hebrew text. The Hebrew words translated "helper" literally mean "a helper corresponding to" the one being helped. Prior to the creation of woman, the man had only animals with which to relate, whereas the focus here is on the unique way humans relate. How empowering it can be for us to realize that this passage emphasizes the equality of two human beings, as opposed to the inequality of humans and animals.

The Hebrew word for "helper" is used sixteen times in Scripture to speak of God's direct assistance to human beings. A word used in reference to God could never describe a secondary status. What does this tell you about yourself?

1. The Old Testament was originally written in Hebrew, the New Testament in Greek.

Then the daughters of Zelophehad came forward.... The names of his daughters were: Mahlah, Noah, Hoglah, Milcah, and Tirzah. They stood before Moses, Eleazar the priest, the leaders, and all the congregation, at the entrance of the tent of meeting, and they said,... "Give to us a possession among our father's brothers." Moses brought their case before the LORD. And the LORD spoke to Moses, saying: "The daughters of Zelophehad are right in what they are saying; you shall indeed let them possess an inheritance among their father's brothers and pass the inheritance of their father on to them."
Numbers 27:1–7

I f you want to open the floodgates of guilt and dissension anywhere in America, start talking about child care," writes Hillary Rodham Clinton in her best-selling book, *It Takes a Village*.[1] The First Lady has raised child care as an issue to be addressed by the federal government, the state, the private sector, and the community. Is such advocacy new?

When their father dies without a male heir in 1260 B.C.E., Zelophehad's daughters present a convincing case before Moses to keep their father's name and inherit his property. In their culture, their actions are bold indeed, exhibiting great strength and courage. Contrary to the laws of the day, the

Lord heartily confirms the women's position. This simple act speaks volumes to me about God's view of women.

Even so, there are still laws in the United States that discriminate against women. For example, Congress has yet to pass an Equal Rights Amendment, and we still do not have a nationally subsidized child-care program.

I used to think advocacy for women's rights began with the women suffragettes in the nineteenth century. How wrong I was! What might happen if women today had the courage of Zelophehad's daughters?

1. Hillary Rodham Clinton, *It Takes a Village* (New York: Simon and Schuster, 1996), 223.

Paul,... To the saints who are in Ephesus:... No one ever hates [their] own body, but...nourishes and tenderly cares for it, just as Christ does for the church.

Ephesians 1:1; 5:29

Are you happy with your body? If you are, you're in a minority of women. Most of us begin at an early age to be ashamed of our bodies. A recent survey found that 53 percent of high school girls are unhappy with their bodies by the age of thirteen; 78 percent are unhappy by the age of eighteen.[1] What's wrong?

First of all, we are bombarded with advertisements that feature extremely tall and thin women. Whereas a generation ago the average model weighed 8 percent less than the average woman, today she weighs 23 percent less.[2]

Women today are given messages that unless they are thin and youthful, their bodies are something to be ashamed of, rather than loved. How instructive it is that we are to love our bodies as much as Christ loves the church—not our thin, svelte bodies, but our bodies, in whatever shape they may be.

How might our lives be different if we loved the body God gave us in the same way Christ loves the church?

1. Naomi Wolf, *The Beauty Myth* (New York: William Morrow, 1991), 185.
2. *Ibid.*, 184.

And the rib that the LORD God had taken from the man he made into a woman and brought her to the man. Then the man said, "This at last is bone of my bones and flesh of my flesh."

Genesis 2:22–23

O dette sat down on the couch in my office and burst into tears. "How can he treat me this way?" she sobbed. "He works twelve hours a day, plays basketball on weekends, and says he's baby-sitting when he takes care of our children. I work full time and do all of the cleaning, then he pats himself on the back when he makes up the bed on Saturday mornings."

If I had a dollar for every time I've heard a version of this story, I could build an incredible women's center with twenty-four-hour counseling. Yet, does Adam predict such arrangements when he first sees Eve?

The Woman's Bible, published in 1895 states, "Adam proclaims the eternal oneness of the happy pair, 'This is at last bone of my bone and flesh of my flesh'; no hint of her subordination. How could men, admitting these words to be divine revelation, ever have preached the subjection of woman?"[1]

Yes, we are indeed flesh of each other's flesh, created by God, for God, and for one another. How can we best remember this in our daily lives?

1. Elizabeth Cady Stanton and the Revising Committee, *The Woman's Bible* (Seattle: Coalition on Women and Religion, 1895, 1974), 21.

The king of Egypt said to the Hebrew midwives, one of whom was named Shiphrah and the other Puah, "When you act as midwives to the Hebrew women, and see them on the birth stool, if it is a boy, kill him; but if it is a girl, she shall live." But the midwives feared God; they did not do as the king of Egypt commanded them, but they let the boys live.

Exodus 1:15–17

I magine the anxiety Shiphrah and Puah feel when they are summoned by their king. They are midwives, slaves, who are suddenly ordered to kill all of the male Hebrew babies. Their purpose in life is to preserve the life of mother and child, yet suddenly they are commanded to become murderers.

Courageously risking their own lives, they defy the king's orders and save the lives of countless male Hebrew babies. Why? Because they know that the king's command is contrary to the laws of God. When the king asks why they have allowed the boys to live, they shrewdly deceive him, and "so God dealt well with the midwives" (v. 20). What inner strength it must have taken for them to act so boldly, in defiance of the king.

Fearlessly challenging unjust structures was a hallmark of the life and ministry of Jesus as well. Could Shiphrah and Puah have been role models for him? What would it take for them to be role models for you?

*For thus says the L*ORD*:... "As a mother comforts her child, so I will comfort you.... You shall see, and your heart shall rejoice."*
Isaiah 66:12–14

Have you ever stopped to wonder who our biblical mothers really are? The great matriarchs of Scripture may come to mind—Sarah, Rebekah, and Rachel. However, our greatest biblical mother of all is God. Numerous times in Scripture God is referred to as a comforting mother, a nursing mother, even a woman in labor. How strange and new these images may seem, yet they were written nearly 3,000 years ago.

Does this mean that God is literally female? Of course not, no more so than God is male, for God is beyond gender. What it does mean is that these images have been there in Scripture all along, to remind you, and to remind me, that as women we are indeed created in the image of God.

Time and again we are told that we can rest in the knowledge that whatever our afflictions, God will be there for us as a comforting mother. How were you comforted as a child? God can do that for you now, and more, much more than you can even ask or imagine.

What might happen if you prayed to God as your comforting mother?

At that time Deborah, a prophetess, wife of Lappidoth, was judging Israel. She used to sit under the Palm of Deborah...and the Israelites came up to her for judgment.

Judges 4:4–5

I can bring home the bacon, fry it up in a pan, and never let you forget you're a man, 'cause I'm a woman...Enjoli." Remember the 1970s television ad that featured a woman in a pin-striped business suit, singing these words as she fried bacon? The idea was that if we purchased Enjoli perfume, we, too, could be so clever.

Well, Deborah never had any Enjoli, but could she ever bring home the bacon and fry it up! Here's a woman who is not only a prophet, mother, and wife, but she is also the only female judge in Scripture and a leader in battle.

When she believes God is calling her to send troops into war, she does so without hesitation. She summons Barak, a general, who says, "If you will go with me, I will go; but if you will not go with me, I will not go." Imagine a general making such a request! Deborah goes, and the troops are victorious.

More than 3,000 years ago, Deborah had a clear sense of her own authority and was comfortable in a leadership role. How might we better accept ourselves as leaders today?

Then the LORD answered Job out of the whirlwind:... "Who shut in the sea with doors when it burst out from the womb?"

Job 38:1, 8

The rise and fall of the tide has always had a mesmerizing effect on me. As I stand at the shoreline, the frothy waves rush almost to my toes and then suddenly retreat, as if beckoning me to follow. Bursting out from God's womb, the sea rushes forth, then quickly recedes. Rhythmically, the advance and retreat of the waves draws me back—back into the womb of the God who gave us birth.

As I stare into the azure waters, which become increasingly darker and deeper near the horizon, I wonder, "Are there secrets in these waters of our birth, clues to God's will for our lives?" The never-ceasing rise and fall, push and pull, remind me that God is never through creating us. At times we need to allow ourselves to drift out into the depths of the sea, into the stiller, deeper waters of our birth to listen, listen, listen to the heart of God. Resting in the womb of God once again, we can find comfort, renewal, and strength.

What secrets might the sea hold for you?

The angel said to her, "Do not be afraid, Mary, for you have found favor with God."

Luke 1:30

I magine you're at home alone, cleaning up the dinner dishes. You're engaged to the most wonderful man you've ever known, and you're dreaming of what married life will be like. Suddenly, someone appears and says, "Greetings, favored one! The Lord is with you" (v. 28). Startled, you wonder if you're still dreaming. Then you're overcome with a paralyzing fear. Should you stay and listen, or run out the door and never look back? What is going on?

Mary's response to the sudden intrusion is much like ours might have been. We are told that, "she was much perplexed by his words and pondered what sort of greeting this might be" (v. 29). Recognizing her fear, the angel comforts her saying, "Do not be afraid."

Do you sometimes feel afraid, wondering what God might have in store for you? I know I have felt this way on a number of occasions. How comforting it is to know that women before us have shared our feelings, even Mary, the mother of Jesus.

"Do not be afraid." Your angels may be saying these same words to you this very moment. Can you hear them?

In those days Mary set out and went with haste to a Judean town in the hill country, where she entered the house of Zechariah and greeted Elizabeth.... And Mary remained with her about three months.

Luke 1:39–40, 56

To be pregnant is one thing. To be pregnant with the Christ is something altogether different. How could this happen? This was not the way Mary had planned her life."[1]

Mary desperately needs to talk with a trusted friend. She suddenly remembers Elizabeth, barren for years, now pregnant with the child who would become John the Baptist. But suppose her kinswoman doesn't believe her? It's a chance Mary has to take, so she leaves "with haste."

There's a great deal of humanity revealed in these two words. Mary doesn't wait to hear the comments of her contemporaries. She doesn't even try to explain everything to Joseph. She knows what she needs—a woman who can understand—so she packs up and leaves. It is three months before Mary returns.

How important our friends can be to us, especially in times of confusion or trouble. When did you last spend time alone with a woman friend?

1. Renita Weems, *Just a Sister Away* (San Diego, Calif.: LuraMedia, 1988), 118.

Then Job answered [God]:... "Did you not pour me out like milk and curdle me like cheese? You clothed me with skin and flesh, and knit me together with bones and sinews. You have granted me life and steadfast love, and your care has preserved my spirit."

Job 9:1; 10:10–12

My husband, Michael, used to spend many memorable hours on his grandparents' farm. He would delight in riding their tractor from sunup to sundown and in eating tomatoes held in his hand like an apple.

Life there revolved around his Grandma Rainey, the matriarch of the family. As a farmer's wife, she spent her days churning cream to make butter, sewing clothes for her children, and knitting into the late afternoon. Over the years she became an icon of maternal love, much beloved by all.

The love and care described here by Job is that of a Hebrew mother for her family—pouring milk, curdling cheese, clothing her children, and knitting. What a wonderful image of God as a homemaker, busily caring for her children.

Today the role of a homemaker is sometimes belittled, yet such tasks are vital to life and preservation of the spirit. Particularly as women, we need to applaud those who have chosen to work primarily in the home.

What would it take for us all to affirm each other's choices?

There was also a prophet, Anna.... She was of a great age.... She never left the temple but worshiped there with fasting and prayer night and day. At that moment she came, and began to praise God and to speak about the child to all who were looking for the redemption of Jerusalem.

Luke 2:36–38

W hen Jesus is eight days old, Mary and Joseph bring him to the temple to be circumcised and designated as holy to the Lord. As they walk into the temple, they spot an old, bent-over woman, one of the regulars who prays and fasts night and day. But Anna is not just any woman; she is a prophet, who immediately recognizes their child as the long-awaited Messiah.

Anna is the first person in Scripture to recognize the true identity of Jesus, and she does so when he is only eight days old! She then wastes no time in proclaiming this good news to all who are looking for the redemption of Jerusalem, which is most likely every Jew in the city. Thus, the first evangelist in all of Scripture is an elderly woman, willing to share her insight with others.

I have often wondered how Anna was received. Did people believe her when she told them a baby would be the savior of their nation? Whatever their reaction, I doubt she allowed it to dampen her enthusiasm.

Have you ever known a person like Anna? What did she share with you?

Moses heard the people weeping throughout their families, all at the entrances of their tents. Then the LORD became very angry, and Moses was displeased. So Moses said to the LORD, "Why have you treated your servant so badly? Why have I not found favor in your sight, that you lay the burden of all this people on me? Did I conceive all this people? Did I give birth to them, that you should say to me, 'Carry them in your bosom, as a nurse carries a suckling child,' to the land that you promised on oath to their ancestors?"

Numbers 11:10–12

On the Exodus journey, Moses becomes weary with the complaining of the Israelites. In frustration, he reminds God that it is God who conceived, carried at the breast, and fed Israel—not him! Why should he be burdened with them now?

In his moment of desperation, Moses turns to God as Mother of the Israelite people. Yet, turning to God as Mother today can be difficult for men and women alike. We have been so immersed in the image of God as Father that other ancient images can seem strange to us. When I first prayed to God as Mother, it felt uncomfortable, so I prayed to "God beyond my naming," hoping that God would give me an image. I have reflected on what happened, in the following poem:

Gentle Guide

O God of many names, God beyond my naming,
Images swirl through my head.
Which ones for me now? Which one will work,
Since "Father" is but one among many?

O Great Patriarch, King of all creation,
Your little girl's not little anymore.
Images are shed before others fill the void
Leaving me vulnerable, raw, and exposed.

How to relate, how to commune
With this new-found, Transcendent Other,
Eluding my grasp, escaping my reach,
Moving like mist through my fingers?

Don't try to force it, just let it come,
Through the Source from which you draw strength.
Breathe in, breathe out, relax, be at peace
And trust in God, your Creator.

"You've sent me a bird? An animal? That's strange!
What am I to do now?"
"Climb up, nestle in, there's a place for you here,
In the down that is under my wing."

Safe and secure, upward we soar,
The sound of the wind rushing by.
Gliding, sailing, new destinies await,
This explorer and her gentle Guide.

—Elizabeth Rankin Geitz

But now thus says the LORD,... "I have called you by name, you are mine."
Isaiah 43:1

I'm forty years old and it's time I figured out who I am," said Jacqueline. We were in her study where her bookshelves were lined with every self-help book and video imaginable. A bright, energetic woman, Jacqueline had held a series of jobs that led nowhere. "I need something that's challenging and fulfilling," she said, "something that will reflect who I am as a person."

Some people read hundreds of books and talk to numerous people to help them figure out who they are. But the search is often in vain, because the basic question is wrong. The question is not, *"Who* am I?" but *"Whose* am I?" The answer? We are God's, first and foremost. We are created in God's image and we belong to God. When we hold this thought close to our hearts, everything else can gradually fall into place.

Whose are you?

Greet Prisca and Aquila, who work with me in Christ Jesus, and who risked their necks for my life.... Greet also the church in their house.
Romans 16:3-5

Prisca and Aquila are a married couple who travel with Saint Paul to spread the gospel. Prisca is an equal part of the ministry team, working side by side with her husband and Saint Paul. What a model they can be to us of women and men working in partnership together. Miriam Therese Winter has written a moving prayer of thanksgiving about their mutual ministry:

We thank You, O God Within and Beyond us, for linking our lives in so many ways, making a chain of hope and compassion long enough and strong enough to circle the globe. When we walk hand in hand, when we work side by side, the impossible becomes the next challenge before us, and we know we can do what we dared not attempt. May mountains of misery melt with Your Word of concern which we put into action, and may there never again be despair or denial of Your saving grace. Amen.[1]

How might Prisca and Aquila's partnership inform your life?

1. Miriam Therese Winter, *WomanWord: A Femisist Lectionary and Psalter on Women of the New Testament* (New York: The Crossroad Publishing Co., 1990), 237.

Moses' father-in-law said to him, "What you are doing is not good. You will surely wear yourself out, both you and these people with you. For the task is too heavy for you; you cannot do it alone."

Exodus 18:17–18

Burnout has become one of the buzzwords of this generation. Hundreds of articles have been written about how to avoid it, how to overcome it, or what to do if you have it. It is touted as a problem of the "yuppie" generation, who want to have it all and do it all, regardless of the personal cost.

How often have you said "yes" to too many tasks and ended up feeling exhausted? As women, this is especially easy for us to do, because we are often wearing many different hats at the same time—daughter, mother, friend, wife, co-worker, housekeeper, and the list goes on. Over time, women have learned to juggle all the demands placed on them, almost too successfully.

As Moses' father-in-law reminded him more than 3,000 years ago, "The task is too heavy for you; you cannot do it alone." Many of us know this intuitively, but find it difficult to ask others for help, or we incorrectly assume that it's easier to do it ourselves.

Are you overworked? Whom can you ask for help?

Paul,... To all God's beloved in Rome:... I commend to you our sister Phoebe, a deacon of the church at Cenchreae, so that you may welcome her in the LORD as is fitting for the saints, and help her in whatever she may require from you, for she has been a benefactor of many and of myself as well.

Romans 1:1, 7; 16:1–2

I n these unique words of commendation, Saint Paul refers to Phoebe as a sister, deacon, and benefactor. The Greek word Saint Paul uses for "deacon" is the same word he uses to describe himself and other church leaders. Thus, he views Phoebe as an equal partner in the gospel. Saint Paul beseeches his readers to extend to her a welcome in the Lord, fitting for the saints. This exemplary woman gives of herself in ministering as a deacon and also gives out of the abundance of her wealth to build up the church.

Women with financial means may at times feel guilty about their position in life. Phoebe shows us that it is not the presence or absence of money that makes a person worthy in the eyes of the Lord, but rather how they use it.

In our society, money equals power. Those who have been blessed with power are called by God to use that power to help the powerless. How might you better use your resources?

Hear the word of the LORD, O people of Israel;... "It was I who taught Ephraim to walk, I took them up in my arms; but they did not know that I healed them."

Hosea 4:1; 11:3

I decided long ago, never to walk in anyone's shadow...." My student, Maria, was softly singing the lyrics of this song as she worked. When she saw me, her eyes brightened. "All my life I've lived in someone else's shadow, and this is where it stops," she exclaimed.

At first it was difficult for Maria to make it to class on a regular basis. She would disappear, then return, determined to turn her life around. Maria was twenty-nine but was emotionally arrested at the age of twelve, when her father began sexually abusing her in front of her mother. No wonder she couldn't quite pull her life together.

I would return to the suburbs after teaching in the inner city and hear remarks such as, "I just don't understand why those women stay on welfare. I'm tired of supporting lazy people." How little they knew about the people they spoke of so judgmentally.

Teaching someone to walk can take many forms. Just as God has taught us to walk and healed us, we are also called to teach others.

Who needs your help to walk again? What might you do for that person?

Then Moses went up to God; the LORD called to him from the mountain, saying,… "You have seen what I did to the Egyptians, and how I bore you on eagles' wings and brought you to myself."

Exodus 19:3–4

Y ou've never seen a mother eagle with her eaglets?" exclaimed my brother Brad to his friend. "Come on, I'll show you a nest." They arrived and waited two hours, but there was no mother eagle in sight. With binoculars, they finally sighted her, carefully watching them, so they moved.

The mother eagle, with food in her talons, then gracefully flew toward her hungry eaglets. But rather than bringing the food to them, she placed it in a nearby tree, forcing them out of the nest. As the first eaglet faltered, the mother eagle flew under it and lifted it up, then dropped away again when the eaglet could fly on its own.

Following the Exodus journey, God tells Moses that God carried the Israelites to safety on eagles' wings. This maternal image of God is that of a mother eagle teaching her young to fly. What a comforting image of our Creator, who is there to lift us when we fall!

What would it feel like to be carried on the wings of God?

But Jesus said to them,... "From the beginning of creation, 'God made them male and female.' "

Mark 10:5–6

Elizabeth, I just don't get it," said Sarah. "I've never felt oppressed in any way." Sarah lived a comfortable suburban life supported by her husband, who had a well-paying job. She had never wanted for anything and enjoyed her many hours of volunteer work each week.

Money can obscure many things. It can close our eyes to the needs of others, as well as to our own inner needs. That which we fail to see can often hurt us the most. For many years I felt like Sarah, until I worked with women on welfare in the inner city. The triple effects of sexism, racism, and classism were starkly before me, and I had no choice but to question my comfortable assumptions.

It is instructive that when Jesus chooses to speak of the creation of man and woman, he quotes from the first creation account in Genesis, when they are both created at the same time, in the image of God. There is nothing said here about woman as created second and therefore somehow inferior. This view of women as equal is consistent with Jesus' treatment of women throughout his ministry.

How do you hear these words of Jesus?

To the woman [God] said,... "Your desire shall be for your husband, and he shall rule over you."

Genesis 3:16

I was wearing one of those petticoats that crinkled when you sat down, along with my best Sunday bonnet. Attending church with my Southern Baptist grandparents was a treat. It could be hot in the summer, but the collective force of a thousand Jesus fans made the air just fine. Never mind that Jesus was portrayed with blond hair and blue eyes. This was the 1950s, when political correctness meant inviting the right politician's wife for tea.

This morning the preacher bellowed, "And your husband shall ruuuuuule over you!" I gave my grandmother a questioning look. "It's in the marriage vows. Obey your husband," she whispered. And indeed it was, but was this what God intended?

It is significant that this statement occurs as a punishment after the Fall, after Adam and Eve eat of the forbidden fruit. It is part of the fallen order, not the created order as God intended. Then, as now, God is working to re-create each one of us and to restore right relationships between us, relationships that are reflective of the original intent of creation.

What aspects of your relationships might benefit from re-creation?

Jesus...said to them,... "You will have pain, but your pain will turn into joy. When a woman is in labor, she has pain, because her hour has come. But when her child is born, she no longer remembers the anguish because of the joy of having brought a human being into the world."

John 16:19–22

"O h, Jesus, do you know how much I hurt? Do you know how bad I feel? Please help me," Stephanie cried aloud. Stephanie was working through difficult childhood issues and had awakened in the middle of the night, sobbing. In her pain she did not pray silently as usual, but prayed aloud.

When Stephanie recounted this story to me, her face was glowing. "You won't believe it," she continued. "He came. No, I didn't see him, but I could feel his presence in a profound and powerful way." What utter joy and peace fills her very soul when her profound pain becomes profound and lasting joy.

To speak of such transformation in the midst of pain, Jesus can think of no better analogy than that of a woman in the throes of labor. The pain of labor is hardly exalted today, but perhaps it should be, for with it comes the greatest gift of all. What a marvelous example Jesus gives us in his last hour.

Have you ever had an experience in your life in which great pain brought about lasting joy? What was that like for you?

[Martha] had a sister named Mary, who sat at the LORD'S feet and listened....
But Martha was distracted by her many tasks; so she came to him and asked,
"LORD, do you not care that my sister has left me to do all the work by myself?
Tell her then to help me." But the LORD answered her, "Martha, Martha, you
are worried and distracted by many things; there is need of only one thing.
Mary has chosen the better part, which will not be taken away from her."
                                                                    Luke 10:39–42

And now for our next story, the mom who went up a tree," said Katie Couric, with a big smile on her face. Suddenly the "Today Show" camera panned to a woman sitting in a tree house, holding a yellow poster that read, "Mom on Strike." Tired of doing all the housework and being taken for granted by her three children, this mom had officially gone on strike. What a woman.

Have you ever longed for an excuse to be liberated from housework? Well, here's one, in the Bible no less! Martha, a homemaker, is busy preparing a meal for Jesus while her sister, Mary, sits and listens at his feet. Whom does Jesus commend? Mary.

In the busyness of our lives, we often fail to take a break for relaxation or intellectual nourishment, yet Jesus urges Martha to do so. Is there a message here for the family of the mom on strike? For you?

When Martha heard that Jesus was coming, she went and met him, while Mary stayed at home. Martha said to Jesus, "LORD, if you had been here, my brother would not have died...." Jesus said to her, "Your brother will rise again." Martha said to him, "I know that he will rise again in the resurrection on the last day." Jesus said to her, "I am the resurrection and the life. Those who believe in me, even though they die, will live.... Do you believe this?" She said to him, "Yes, LORD, I believe that you are the Messiah, the Son of God, the one coming into the world."

John 11:20–27

T he Gospel of John presents us with a different view of Martha, whose brother, Lazarus, has been dead for four days. Here Martha is outspoken, somewhat stubborn, and passionate about her faith. Most important, she responds to Jesus with the affirmation that he is the Christ. The only other verbal confession of Jesus as the Christ is made by Peter in the Gospel of Matthew. In the early church, confessing Jesus as the Christ was the mark of an apostle, yet it is only Peter's confession that has been highlighted in the tradition of the church.

Let's celebrate Martha's matter-of-fact approach to life, her willingness to argue theologically with Jesus, and most important, her insight into the true identity of Jesus.

Are you ever afraid to share your perspective when it differs from those around you? As often the only woman in a group of Episcopal priests, I used to hesitate to voice my views when they were different, but not any longer. My biblical mothers and sisters have become great role models for me.

When you feel like holding back, what might happen if you remembered Martha?

And God said to them, "...Have dominion over the fish of the sea and over the birds of the air and over every living thing that moves upon the earth."
Genesis 1:28

"G igantic Goldfish Discovered," read the headline in 1961. I could hardly believe our discovery was worthy of an article in the local newspaper. Several years before, my brothers and I had released our pet goldfish, Gus, into our neighbor's pond. Then one day we spied Gus—all 12 inches of him! We quickly caught him in a bucket and took him home to our aquarium.

Several months went by, and we noticed that Gus seemed listless. He even seemed to be getting smaller. To save him, we returned him to the pond, where he could grow again, independent of our dominion over him.

Historically, the Bible has been used to justify the dominion of man over woman. Yet, in Genesis, after the first creation account, of both male and female in the image of God, God gives them both dominion over every living creature. Nothing is said here giving either sex dominion over the other.

What a positive reminder that women and men are meant to live in equal partnership. How can we best weave the delicate thread of true partnership into our relationships today?

Thus says the LORD:... "Can a woman forget her nursing child, or show no compassion for the child of her womb? Even these may forget, yet I will not forget you."

Isaiah 49:8

R ocking and nursing a tiny infant in the silence of the night can be an experience of near sacred dimensions. Mother and child seem almost as one, as the chair rocks slowly to and fro. This little bundle, dependent upon us for its very existence, holds our very life and sustenance within it. As the infant snuggles close for warmth, comfort, and food, we find ourselves basking in the glow. The tenderness and compassion of that moment is nevertheless eclipsed by God's overwhelming love and compassion for us.

In the midst of our busy lives it is easy to forget that God loves us with a love that knows no bounds. It is easy to forget that everything we do is supported by God's unconditional love for us.

"I will not forget you," God says. Through trials and tribulations, joys and sorrows, we are resting in the palm of God's hand, comfortably cradled in the arms of the God who gave us birth.

How might your life be different if you could allow yourself to feel the strength of God's love for you each day?

Paul,...To the church...in Corinth:... For God's temple is holy, and you are that temple.

1 Corinthians 1:1–2; 3:17

I went to work out at the gym yesterday after a three-month break. "Where have you been?" asked Donnette. "Enjoying life," I replied. "Did you exercise at all while you were away?" "Nope." "Were you sick or anything?" "Nope." "But you didn't exercise at all." "Nope." There was a pregnant silence as she tried to figure out the motivation, or lack thereof, in yet another middle-aged client. "I must confess," I added, "I enjoy the life of a couch potato."

Well, it's true. One of my favorite T-shirts says, "Eat right. Exercise. Die Anyway." It's also true that I have another one that says, "It took me 40 years to look this good." It's usually a toss-up as to which slogan will win out on any given day, and, no, I won't tell you how old the second T-shirt is!

What does it mean that we are God's temple, as Saint Paul tells us? If our bodies are the dwelling place of the Holy One, it matters greatly to God what we do with our bodies. Overeating, smoking, drinking to excess, or never exercising— all have long-term effects on our health and well-being.

Is this how we are meant to treat God's temple? What small change might you make in the way you treat your body?

Hear what the LORD says:... "*I sent before you Moses, Aaron, and Miriam.*"
Micah 6:1, 4
Then the prophet Miriam, Aaron's sister, took a tambourine in her hand; and all the women went out after her with tambourines and with dancing.
Exodus 15:20

W hen Moses leads the Israelites out of bondage in Egypt toward the promised land, he is not alone. His sister, Miriam, and his brother, Aaron, are also sent by God to lead the Exodus. All three of them are identified as leaders. Has someone else ever gotten all of the recognition for something in which you played a significant role? This is what happened to Miriam and Aaron.

Not only does Miriam save Moses' life as a child and help lead the Exodus, but she also is designated in Scripture as a prophet, indicating that she is held in high esteem by her community. Lifesaver, leader, and prophet—Miriam is indeed a remarkable and versatile woman.

Miriam is also wise enough to celebrate their Exodus victory by leading the women in dancing and shaking tambourines. Miriam knows how to have fun and celebrate a victory. Why is it that we often forget to celebrate our victories? Can you celebrate one of yours with a friend?

If I have repaid my friend with harm or plundered my enemy without cause,
then let the enemy pursue and overtake me, trample my life to the ground,
and lay my soul in the dust.

Psalm 7:4–5

Do we dare pray these words of the psalmist? How tempting it is to repay harm with harm, but truly we are never further from God than when we do so. The inability to forgive someone who has betrayed us or hurt us deeply can rob us of the joy of living, imprisoning us in a cage of our own making. Over time, the bars become stronger and therefore harder to break, hurting not only us, but all those who love us.

Although it is appropriate to feel anger toward someone who has hurt us, it is not healthy for us to get stuck in these feelings for a prolonged period of time. Praying for our enemies can stop this vicious cycle of hurt and woundedness, freeing us from negative thoughts and energies, moving us toward greater communion with God.

For whom do you find it difficult to pray? What might happen if you asked God's grace to fill your heart so that you might pray for this person?

So Jacob arose, and set his children and his wives on camels.... Now Laban had gone to shear his sheep, and Rachel stole her father's household gods.... Now Rachel had taken the household gods and put them in the camel's saddle, and sat on them. Laban felt all about in the tent, but did not find them. And she said to her father, "Let not my LORD be angry that I cannot rise before you, for the way of women is upon me." So he searched, but did not find the household gods.

Genesis 31:17–19, 34–35

Jacob works for seven long years to secure the hand of Laban's daughter, Rachel, in marriage. However, Laban deceives Jacob by disguising his other daughter, Leah, as Rachel and tricks Jacob into marrying her instead. One week later, Jacob is allowed to marry Rachel, which sets up a rivalry between the two sisters that never ends.

Before leaving for Canaan with Jacob, Leah, and all their children, Rachel steals her father's household gods and successfully hides them, keeping them for herself. Rachel shamelessly stands up to patriarchal power, which has been used against her, and seizes it for herself. She then ironically uses that which is considered a woman's curse to keep it in her possession. Turning a negative into a positive is a strength in any age. Here's to Rachel!

What negative in your life might be turned into a positive?

"When you pass through the waters, I will be with you; and through the rivers, they shall not overwhelm you; when you walk through fire you shall not be burned.... For I am the LORD your God."

Isaiah 43:2–3

I once saw a cartoon of a large fish attempting to swallow a penguin, as another penguin looks on and says, "Relax. God's in charge." Sometimes it's hard to believe God's in charge when the floodgates burst open. But this is what God affirms throughout Scripture—not that at times we won't feel overwhelmed, but that in those times God will be with us.

Have you ever longed for the comfort of God's presence, but couldn't feel it, regardless of how hard you tried? Some people call this experience the absence of God; I prefer to call it the hiddenness of God, for even when we can't feel God's presence, God is still there.

When I feel abandoned by God, I often find that I am the one putting up the roadblocks. Perhaps it is anger at God, or another unresolved issue, that is getting in the way. Whatever the cause, when I am able to work through it, I often find that God suddenly reappears, for God has never left.

How would it feel to know that God is with you in every difficult situation?

Hear the word of the L<small>ORD</small>, O people of Israel:... "I was to them like those who lift infants to their cheeks. I bent down to them and fed them."
Hosea 4:1; 11:4

Motherhood, *the Second Oldest Profession*, reads the title of an Erma Bombeck book. I've always chuckled when I've seen that title, and until recently I thought it was true. Today I'm not so sure, for who is God, if not our biblical mother? God is described in Scripture as groaning in labor, giving birth to creation, and nursing us at the breast. In addition, Hosea tells us that God feels as tender toward the Israelites as those who lift infants to their cheeks. In biblical times it was only the mother who could feed an infant.

In reality, human mothers may not always be so tender and loving. Mothers are children of God who have their own wounds and hurts. They may try with all their hearts to love their children unconditionally, yet if they have never experienced that love themselves, it will be difficult. Therefore, women need the image of God as a mother, not only to see ourselves as created in God's image, but also to compensate for the frailty of human parents.

Motherhood, the oldest profession, perfected by God for you and for me. What might happen if you let God lift you and feed your spiritual needs?

After leaving the synagogue [Jesus] entered Simon's house. Now Simon's mother-in-law was suffering from a high fever, and they asked him about her. Then he stood over her and rebuked the fever, and it left her.

Luke 4:38–39

I n the Gospel of Luke, the first person healed by Jesus is Simon Peter's mother-in-law. Many rabbis of his time would not heal women, but Jesus did so time and again.

Throughout my ministry, I have been privileged to witness the healing power of the risen Christ in many people's lives. During a particularly difficult time in my own life, I, too, experienced powerfully Christ's healing power. I have written about my experience in the following poem. Come share that morning with me…

If you were to ask the risen Christ to heal one wound that you carry, what would it be?

Easter Mourning

The smell of lilies permeates my senses
As alleluias ring through the air.
"Rejoice. Christ is risen. Yes, risen indeed!"
Yet for me, I'm still on Golgotha.

Weeping, kneeling at the foot of the cross
Wounds bleeding, water flowing
to mesh with my tears.
Ashes to ashes, dust to dust
But not now, not here, not this way!

"My God, my God, why have you forsaken me?"
O Wounded One, don't leave me, not now.
My pain is your pain and your pain is mine.
Flesh rips, hearts bleed, then it stops.

Now I'll carry you, as you've carried me
Giving birth to the you now within me.
Hearts mingle, tears spill as my love overflows
For the Wounded One, Risen One,
life-giving Lover of Souls.
—Elizabeth Rankin Geitz

Paul, Silvanus, and Timothy, To the church of the Thessalonians:... We were gentle among you, like a nurse tenderly caring for her own children.... You have become very dear to us.

1 Thessalonians 1:1; 2:7–8

Pat Johnson had served as a nurse in Vietnam for several months when she requested a transfer to a MASH hospital. They assigned her to the emergency room, where she often worked sixteen-hour shifts. Each day many brave young men came in, really hurting, really afraid, and gravely wounded.

She tells us: "I used to wonder if the families of the kids who died there knew that there were people who really cared about their kids and were doing all the extra-special things that they would have done if they were there. Looking back, I see my role probably the best as having felt a lot of compassion for these kids and trying to let them know we really cared about them."[1]

When Saint Paul, Silvanus, and Timothy want to express the tenderness they feel for the church of Thessalonica, they compare themselves to a nurse much like Pat. What a powerful image of selfless love and compassion!

What clues might this give us regarding Saint Paul's view of women?

1. Keith Walker, *A Piece of My Heart: The Stories of Twenty-six American Women Who Served in Vietnam* (New York: Ballantine Books, 1985), 57.

[Rebekah's] brother and her mother said, "Let the girl remain with us a while, at least ten days; after that she may go." But he said to them, "Do not delay me."... They said, "We will call the girl, and ask her. And they called Rebekah, and said to her, "Will you go with this man?" She said, "I will."

Genesis 24:55–58

A t the time the Bible was written, all marriages were arranged, with the woman having no say in the choice of her husband. After marriage a woman became the property of the man and was treated as such.

When it comes time for his son Isaac to marry, Abraham sends his servant to find an appropriate wife for Isaac. He meets Rebekah and asks her father, Bethuel, for her hand in marriage. Bethuel immediately gives his consent. However, Rebekah's brother and mother refuse. They radically break with tradition and ask Rebekah whether she wants to go, before sending her away to marry a complete stranger.

Rebekah's father assumes she will obey his word and leave for a foreign country to marry a man she has never seen. Such assumptions are rarely made today, but other assumptions are made about women's lives.

Did something similar occur in your life? What effect did it have on you?

I the LORD speak the truth.... "Listen to me, O house of Jacob...who have been borne by me from your birth, carried from the womb; even to your old age I am he, even when you turn gray I will carry you. I have made, and I will bear; I will carry and will save."

Isaiah 45:19; 46:3–4

T he hardest job in the world is doing nothing," lamented Nancy Hodges, a spry ninety-year-old. With a frail body, but an alert mind, she is a delightful conversation partner who still lives alone. "I can't get out anymore, but, oh, how my church friends take care of me. I'm not comfortable with it, but I don't know what I'd do without them," she says, as her eyes fill with tears.

As we grow older, we may not feel comfortable with the image of being carried like a child. Yet God tells us that not only are we carried from the womb as infants, but God continues to carry us when we are old and gray. We are never too old to be held in the arms of God. From womb to tomb God carries us. Sometimes God works through other people, like Nancy's friends; at other times we can almost feel the arms of God surrounding us and lifting us up.

Have you ever felt that you were being carried in the arms of God? How did it feel?

Then the woman came and told her husband, "A man of God came to me, and his appearance was like that of an angel of God, most awe-inspiring."... The angel of God came again to the woman as she sat in the field; but her husband Manoah was not with her.

Judges 13:6, 9

An angel appears to Manoah's wife to tell her that she will conceive and bear a son. She immediately recognizes her visitor as an angel of God and reports this visitation to her husband. The angel then visits her again, and she brings Manoah to him, so that he too might believe. Even so, "Manoah did not know that he was the angel of the LORD" (v. 16).

Manoah's wife trusts her intuition and acts on it, putting her trust in the LORD. Human reason might have told her that her visitor could not possibly be an angel, but she listens to her heart instead. After believing God's messenger, she gives birth to their long-awaited child, Samson.

Today we may hear God's message for us in any number of ways—through trusted friends, relatives, strangers, or the still, small voice within us. We are all called to listen to God's word for us, wherever we may find it.

What if we, like Manoah's wife, could trust our intuition and respond accordingly?

Then [Jesus] began to speak:... "Therefore I tell you, do not worry about your life.... Can any of you by worrying add a single hour to your span of life?"
Matthew 5:2; 6:25, 27

As a teenager, my brother Lane was an avid subscriber to *Mad* magazine. Each issue contained a picture of the inimitable hero, Alfred E. Neuman, with his slogan, "What, me worry?" How I envied the Alfred E. Neumans of the world, and still do, for worrying is second nature to me.

"Don't trouble trouble, till trouble troubles you" is a wonderful maxim, but one I couldn't seem to put into practice. Regardless of how hard I tried, I still worried, expending much needless time and energy.

Fortunately, somewhere along my spiritual journey I finally realized that the opposite of worrying is not the absence of worry, but the presence of trust—trust in God. How can we worry about the future if we truly put our lives in God's hands? We can't.

The simple phrase "Let go and let God" can change the fabric of our days, but it isn't always easy to incorporate into our lives. Letting go of something small is a good way to begin.

What in your life do you need to let go of and put into the hands of God?

O LORD,…I have calmed and quieted my soul, like a weaned child with its mother; my soul is like the weaned child that is with me.
Psalm 131:1,2

Growing up can be a confusing process. At times we may feel a force pulling us toward new horizons, while another draws us close to the familiar. The growth process can be difficult, because shedding the old and embracing the new requires a willingness to be vulnerable.

Just ask the California spiny lobster. In order to grow, it must shed its hard outer shell, leaving its new, soft skin completely vulnerable to prey. Yet only when its old shell is discarded can the lobster grow into full maturity.

As the psalmist tells us, there are times in our spiritual lives when we are meant to be like a nursing child, others when we are meant to wean ourselves and grow into maturity, shedding the old to embrace the new. Have you ever known someone who refused to grow up, preferring to be the child in all situations? Yes, we are all God's children, but we are not meant to remain childlike; rather, our souls must be weaned from infant milk.

From what does your soul need to be weaned? What shell might you discard?

David said to Abigail, "Blessed be the LORD, the God of Israel, who sent you to meet me today! Blessed be your good sense, and blessed be you, who have kept me today from bloodguilt and from avenging myself by my own hand!"... Then David...said to her, "Go up to your house in peace; see, I have heeded your voice, and I have granted your petition."

1 Samuel 25:32–35

In the midst of a major conflict, Abigail's wit and initiative save the life of her husband, Nabal, and his men. How did it all start? David has protected Nabal's shepherds, so he asks for a gift of food in return. Being "so ill-natured that no one can speak to him"(v. 17), Nabal refuses. In anger, David prepares his men for battle.

Abigail responds quickly and effectively. Without her husband's knowledge, she has her donkeys laden with food, then rides off to meet David on a mission of peace. Abigail valiantly persuades David to accept the food and stop the attack. Whereas David's immediate response to Nabal's refusal is, "Every man strap on his sword!" (v. 13), Abigail's response is to undertake a mission of peace.

Similar differences between men and women are sometimes seen in the workplace today. A seasoned female attorney writes: "I think that aggressiveness is tolerated and encouraged by men; they're used to doing it. They're expected to do it." She goes on to explain how different her upbringing has been as a female.[1]

How might we, like Abigail, remain true to our strengths without being caught up in the dominant ethos of competitiveness in our world today?

1. Beth Milwid, *Working with Men: Women in the Workplace Talk About Sexuality, Success, and Their Male Coworkers* (New York: Berkley Books, 1990), 147.

"In the last days it will be," God declares, "that I will pour out my Spirit upon all flesh, and your sons and your daughters shall prophesy."
                                                                    Acts 2:17

I've been seeing Margaret Guenther as my spiritual director for the last ten years. She usually wears all black with her priest's collar, her silver hair pulled back in a bun. Her wrinkled face exudes warmth and motherly love, not only for me but also for the many priests throughout the years who have sought the wisdom of her counsel. "Where is God in all of this?" she has often asked in one of our sessions, and together we would figure it out.

Is Margaret a prophet? I would say so. Over the years, she has been able to listen to what I have to say, then help me chart a course that avoids possible pitfalls. She seems to see into the future of the small things in our lives with remarkable clarity, while staying firmly grounded in the present.

The prophetic voice of women has echoed throughout the centuries. A number of women in Scripture are named as prophets—Miriam, Deborah, Huldah, Noadiah, Anna, the unnamed woman in Isaiah, and Philip's daughters.

Has a woman ever had a prophetic role in your life? Can you hear her words to you now?

So the priest Hilkiah, Ahikam, Achbor, Shaphan, and Asaiah went to the prophetess Huldah the wife of Shallum,...where they consulted her.
                                                                    2 Kings 22:14

Huldah was a prophet who, along with the prophet Jeremiah, lived in Jerusalem during the reign of King Josiah in the year 627 B.C.E. When the king discovers the Book of the Law, he commands several men, including the priest Hilkiah, to inquire of the LORD concerning the words of the book. To whom do they turn? Huldah, who interprets the Scriptures for them.

Over the years I have been involved in numerous women's Bible study groups. Each week women of different generations have gathered to support and challenge one another to hear God's word for them revealed through Scripture. The collective wisdom of these women has surrounded me in times of great joy and deep sadness. Together we learned that our issues and problems were not new to our generation. Each and every one had a correlation in Scripture that helped us on our journeys toward wholeness.

The older women were particularly insightful. Have you ever consulted a wise woman like Huldah to interpret Scripture for you? Did her interpretation shed new light on God's word for you?

Paul,... To the church of God that is in Corinth:... Now there are varieties of gifts, but the same Spirit; and there are varieties of services, but the same Lord; and there are varieties of activities, but it is the same God who activates all of them in everyone. To each is given the manifestation of the Spirit for the common good.

1 Corinthians 1:1–2; 12:4–7

A dear friend once sent me a card that said, "What you are is God's gift to you. What you make of yourself is your gift to God." When we focus on our gifts, we need to look at these two aspects of our giftedness—what God has already given to us and what we can give to God in return.

What special gifts has God given you? If you're like most people, you haven't really thought about it, or you may be certain that you have some gifts and not others. One way to test this out is in community. Ask your family and friends what they perceive your gifts to be, then ponder this question: What gifts am I most often asked to use? Saint Paul was clear that our gifts were not given to us for individual use or glory; rather, they were given for the common good.

For the moment, focus on just one special gift God has given you. How might you use it for the common good?

You were unmindful of the Rock that bore you; you forgot the God who gave you birth.

Deuteronomy 32:18

When my grandfather was born, the airplane had not yet been invented. By the time he died, Americans had walked on the moon. When I was a child, we had three black-and-white television stations. Now we have more than a hundred and can watch world news literally as it is happening. When my own children were born, very few people had home computers. Many people now regularly surf the Net and can communicate instantly by e-mail anywhere in the world.

Our lives change, people change, the world around us changes at an alarming speed, but God is as steadfast and steady as a boulder—always constant, always there. The image of God as our Rock can be comforting when it seems that nothing in life is stable or steadfast.

Yet as we are reminded here, we often forget our Rock. Why did God, the Rock of our salvation, give us birth? To serve the God who gave us life with whatever gifts the Lord has given us.

What might happen if you let God be your Rock today?

Hannah rose and presented herself before the LORD.... *She was deeply distressed and prayed to the* LORD, *and wept bitterly.... And the* LORD *remembered her.*

1 Samuel 1:9-10, 19

As a hospital chaplain in training to be a priest, I was suddenly awakened at 6:00 A.M. and called into a patient's room. There lay a woman named Flora who was about to undergo open-heart surgery. "Pray for me, preacher. Pray for me. God has abandoned me. I haven't been going to church, so I don't have any right to be calling on the Lord; but, oh, do I need God now."

I put my hand on her arm and prayed aloud, then we sat together in silence. Suddenly she said, "He's here." I looked up expecting to see the doctor. "No, no," she said. "Jesus is here! He hasn't deserted me. God is sure smiling on me, preacher. God is smiling on me."

In our passage from Samuel, Hannah is distraught to the point of not wanting to eat because she is unable to conceive a child. Her husband and friends try to console her, but to no avail. She then prays, trusting that God will hear her. She prays without ceasing, never gives up, and God smiles on Hannah. She later gives birth to Samuel.

What can we learn from Flora and Hannah?

A Samaritan woman came to draw water, and Jesus said to her, "Give me a drink." (His disciples had gone to the city to buy food.) The Samaritan woman said to him, "How is that you, a Jew, ask a drink of me, a woman of Samaria?"... Then the woman left her water jar and went back to the city. She said to the people, "Come and see a man who told me everything I have ever done!"... Many Samaritans from that city believed in him because of the woman's testimony.

John 4:7–9, 28–29, 39

A trip to the well in Jesus' day was something like a trip to the neighborhood grocery store in our time. Women often gathered there to socialize with one another as they drew bucket after bucket of water. This ritual was part of the rhythm of their lives, at once familiar and life-giving. Imagine the Samaritan woman's surprise when Jesus speaks to her! Not only were men not allowed to speak to women in public, but Jews never spoke to Samaritans.

In the course of their conversation, Jesus tells this rather plucky woman that she has had no less than five husbands and that she is living with a man to whom she is not married. As a result, the woman recognizes Jesus as a prophet. Filled with enthusiasm, she leaves the well so quickly that she forgets her bucket. Immediately, she tells her fellow Samaritans about Jesus, converting many.

What does this encounter reveal about Jesus' acceptance of all women?

"I have been the LORD your God ever since the land of Egypt.... I will fall upon them like a bear robbed of her cubs."

Hosea 13:4, 8

O ne sunny day my husband, children, and I were swimming in the pond on our farm. When the children weren't pushing us off our rafts, Michael and I were lazily drifting in the water. Suddenly, we saw what we thought was an alligator!

We hurried the children out of the pond, only to discover that the "alligator" was a mother bear submerged in the water with just the tip of her back and nose showing. The 500-pound bear emerged and ran to her cubs, who had been in hiding. She then guided them to safety in the surrounding woods.

Mother bears have tremendous affection for their cubs, at times holding them close for comfort, at other times fighting for their protection or guiding them to safety. The image of God as a mother bear is one of my favorites. Yes, we have a God who comforts us, fights for us, and guides us to safety.

What might happen if you called on Mother Bear to protect you?

*On the seventh day, when the king [Ahasuerus] was in good humor, he
told...the seven eunuchs...to escort the queen to him in order to proclaim her
as queen,....and to have her display her beauty to all the governors and the
people of various nations, for she was indeed a beautiful woman. But Queen
Vashti refused to obey him.... This offended the king and he became furious.*
                                                              Esther 1:10–12

A fter much wine has been consumed at a lavish party that lasts for seven
days, King Ahasuerus summons his eunuchs to escort the queen to him to
display her beauty to the men at the gathering. Customarily, the woman was presented without her clothes on. Not surprisingly, the queen adamantly refuses.

As a result, King Ahasuerus refuses to crown her as queen, so that "all women
will give honor to their husbands" (v. 20) and will never follow the queen's
example. Her behavior is viewed as a disgraceful aberration and an embarrass-
ment to the king, whose wife obviously refuses to obey him. At a time when
wives were the property of men, her refusal to comply with patriarchal power
sends shock waves throughout the kingdom. Queen Vashti is a sterling example
of a courageous woman who is willing to face the consequences of her decisions,
regardless of what they may be.

Do you know anyone who has taken a strong stand at great cost to herself?
Is there an area in which you need to be empowered to do so?

Then Esther gave the messenger this answer to take back to Mordecai: "Go and gather all the Jews who are in Susa and fast on my behalf,...and my maids and I will also go without food. After that I will go to the king, contrary to the law, even if I must die."

Esther 4:15–16

Queen Vashti is replaced by another equally strong woman, Queen Esther, who is Jewish. Without the king's knowledge, the king's chief courtier, Haman, orders the execution of all Jews in the kingdom. The king doesn't know Esther is Jewish, so she agonizes over whether to reveal her true identity.

Esther prays to God to save her from her fear, and her prayers are answered. At great risk to herself she decides to reveal her identity. She tells the king, "Let my life be granted me at my petition, and my people at my request. For we have been sold, I and my people, to be destroyed" (7:3–4). As a result of her own willingness to be vulnerable, all the Jews in the kingdom are saved.

Have you ever been afraid to reveal something about yourself? It took me several years to speak publicly of my mother's suicide for fear of what others might think. Yet when I did so, I experienced a freedom that was life-giving.

Are you harboring anything that needs to be brought into the light and shared with others? If so, what might happen if you had the courage of Esther?

Paul an apostle,... To the churches of Galatia:...My little children, for whom I am again in the pain of childbirth until Christ is formed in you, I wish I were present with you now.

Galatians 1:1–2; 4:19–20

Before there were hospitals, antibiotics, Lamaze, and natural childbirth, there was *very* natural childbirth. Most women gave birth at home under rudimentary conditions, with only hot water to kill germs and old rags for cleanup. As a result, throughout the centuries numerous women have died giving birth.

Giving one's life that another human being might live was a painfully familiar process in the lives of women in Saint Paul's day. Thus, when Saint Paul speaks here of being in the pain of childbirth, he is also referring to his willingness to die that others might live into the fullness of the gospel. How unlikely his imagery seems to us today; yet how moving and affirming it is of all things feminine.

When we envision the pain of childbirth in a hospital setting, we first-world women can easily miss the richness and sense of sacrifice embodied in this passage. Saint Paul, as well as many apostles, were willing to die, and did die, that the gospel might live.

What does this mean to you? What could it mean?

But the Lord answered him and said,... "Ought not this woman, a daughter of Abraham,...be set free from this bondage on the Sabbath day?"
Luke 13:15–16

When Jesus is teaching in the synagogue, he sees a woman who has been crippled for eighteen years. He calls her to him, lays hands on her, and heals her. He then refers to her as a daughter of Abraham, an unusual honorific in his own day as well as in ours. Jesus sets this woman free from a bondage that has crippled her for many years.

In my ministry I sometimes see people who are emotionally in bondage. Some have never been able to forgive themselves for something they have done; others can't forgive someone who has hurt them. Still others have experienced a traumatic, or tragic, event in life that they have never been able to work through. In such cases, people can seem to *become* their problems. Their entire life can focus on this one event until they see themselves as permanent victims. I remind them that one event, or even a series of events, does not define their life. It does not define who they are, and certainly not who they can become.

Is anything holding you in bondage today? What do you need to set you free?

When the Lord saw [the widow], he had compassion for her and said to her, "Do not weep."

Luke 7:13

H ughy's well-worn leather halter arrived in the mail in a small cardboard box. What a struggle it had been to try to save the horse's life. Our daughter, Charlotte, loved Hughy with all her heart. He was her life, and now he was dead. As a nine-year-old, she had a dream to compete nationally. Training for three, sometimes six, hours a day for eight years, she had at last qualified for the nationals. Then suddenly, without warning, Hughy contracted pleuroipneumonia and began a slow, painful descent toward death.

When Jesus unexpectedly encounters the funeral procession of a widow's only son, he feels great compassion for her and miraculously raises him from the dead. What I would have given for such a miracle. How helpless I felt.

As Charlotte's family and friends surrounded her with love, it suddenly dawned on me that we weren't the only ones around her. Jesus was also there, filled with compassion, comforting her and saying, "Do not weep." Suddenly, I no longer felt so helpless.

Have you ever longed for our Lord's compassion to surround you when you, or a loved one, were weeping? What would that feel like for you?

Jesus said,... "Truly I tell you, wherever the good news is proclaimed in the whole world, what she has done will be told in remembrance of her."
Mark 14:6, 9

While Jesus is dining in Bethany at the home of Simon the leper, a woman breaks into the room carrying an alabaster jar. She then anoints Jesus' head with a very costly ointment. As a result, she is scolded by several of the men at the dinner, to which Jesus replies, "Let her alone; why do you trouble her?" (v. 6).

Her anointing can be viewed as a prophetic recognition of Jesus as the Christ, since a Messiah would receive such an anointing. So significant is her action to Jesus that he wants her to be remembered wherever the gospel is proclaimed in all the world. What an affirmation of her gift!

Elisabeth Schüssler Fiorenza has written a marvelous book, *In Memory of Her*, about this forgotten woman's courageous act. Since many other memorable women have been forgotten throughout the history of the church, I believe it is our duty to keep their stories alive.

How can we affirm women in our own time who take courageous stands in the face of those who might disagree?

It was you [God] who took me from the womb; you kept me safe on my mother's breast.

Psalm 22:9

I t's a girl!" said the doctor as she handed Josie her tiny, wrinkled, screaming infant. Josie and Alex burst into tears as they finally held their wondrous little creature of God.

They had come to see me several years before, convinced that they would never have children. Josie had experienced three miscarriages and one stillbirth. The couple's hopes and dreams had been shattered again and again. When Josie became pregnant for the fifth time, the entire Christian community prayed diligently for the safe delivery of their baby. When Josie was confined to complete bed rest for the last three months of her pregnancy, her friends from church cheerfully brought her dinner, did the grocery shopping, and helped out with minor household chores.

With the help of the entire Christian community, God literally midwifed that baby to birth. The psalmist here images God as a midwife who takes each one of us from the womb, then keeps us safe on our mother's breast.

In what area of your life do you need to let God be your midwife, bringing new life to birth within you?

A certain woman named Lydia, a worshiper of God, was listening to us; she was from the city of Thyatira and a dealer in purple cloth. The Lord opened her heart to listen eagerly to what was said by Paul. When she and her household were baptized, she urged us, saying, "If you have judged me to be faithful to the Lord, come and stay at my home." And she prevailed upon us.
Acts 16:14–15

"I f Lydia did it, then so can I," said Peggy, as she carried her lay ministry workbook in one hand and a briefcase in the other. To be sure, Lydia knew how to successfully handle competing demands on her time. She was a businesswoman who traded in purple goods, which were luxury items; she helped start the Christian church in Philippi, and she still had time to extend hospitality to Peter and Paul. How did she do it all?

We are told that "the Lord opened her heart to listen eagerly to what was said by Paul." When our hearts are open, we can receive God's endless love for us. Operating from a firm foundation of love, we can then share that love with others. In addition, when we live with the daily realization of God's supportive care for us, we can put our burdens in the hands of the Lord.

When you feel as if you're juggling too much, can you let go and let God? What might happen if you gave God one of your burdens to carry today?

"Listen to me, O house of Jacob, all the remnant of the house of Israel, who have been borne by me from your birth, carried from the womb;...I have made, and I will bear; I will carry and will save.... For I am God, and there is no other."

Isaiah 46:3–4, 9

I've been taking care of folks since I was eight," reflected Annie Harris. Even though she was the youngest child in the family, Annie lovingly took care of her father, brothers, and cousins after her mother became ill.

Annie has made caring for others her life's work. Although she's never literally midwifed a child to birth, she has been a midwife to countless people—children at her day-care center, her own children and grandchildren, extended family, and neighborhood children. No job is too difficult for Annie.

"How do you do it all?" I asked her one afternoon. "Each day I pray for God to give me the strength to help others," she quietly replied. "I'm willing to help anyone God sends my way."

What a wonderful image Annie has given me of God as a midwife. Not only does God bring us to birth, but God still carries us and saves us throughout our lives. There is no load too heavy for God.

What do you need to let God carry for you?

For all of us make many mistakes.

James 3:2

"How could I make such a terrible mistake?" lamented Constance. "My daughter's athletic banquet was last night and I completely forgot about it. I ended up working overtime instead. How will I ever make it up to her?" she said, with tears in her eyes.

The Book of James tells us, very simply, "For all of us make many mistakes." Not some of us, but all of us. How I wish I could remember this when, like Constance, I get frustrated with myself for being human. I often find it easier to forgive others' mistakes than to forgive my own.

As women, we are especially vulnerable to this type of thinking. The media has convinced us that "we've come a long way, baby," and we can have it all. Super achievement is lauded, while mistakes are something to be ashamed of rather than learned from. Instead, honest mistakes should be heralded as important signposts on our journey toward growth and wholeness.

Can you embrace your mistakes today, joyfully accepting them as part of your humanity?

As [Hagar] sat opposite [her son], she lifted up her voice and wept. And God heard the voice of the boy; and the angel of God called to Hagar from heaven, and said to her, "What troubles you, Hagar? Do not be afraid; for God has heard the voice of the boy where he is."

Genesis 21:16–17

The day after the Rodney King verdict, I was with a group of seminarians who marched, sang, and chanted, "No Justice. No Peace." Suddenly I felt the "peace that passes all understanding," for surrounding me were my sisters and brothers in Christ who were Latino, Korean, Japanese, Black, and White. Some were American. Some had come here to study from other countries. All were concerned over the long-term, underlying racial tensions in our country.

Hagar is Sarah and Abraham's slave who, at Sarah's request, conceives and bears Abraham's first son, Ishmael. Subsequently, Sarah becomes pregnant and gives birth to Isaac. After Hagar has served her purpose, Sarah severely mistreats her, and Hagar runs away with Ishmael. Fearing for her child's life, Hagar prays to God; her prayers are answered by an angelic visitation.

The mistreatment of people based on race or class did not begin with our own time, but could it end? Is there one action you could take that might bring people of different races in closer harmony with one another?

Paul an apostle,... To the churches of Galatia:... "God...set me apart from the womb of my mother and called me through his grace."
Galatians 1:1–2, 15

"Our Father, who art in heaven, hallowed be your name." The Reverend Walt Zelley was leading an adult forum on the Lord's Prayer. "Should I tell him he made a mistake?" asked Michael, our ten-year-old son. "What do you mean?" I whispered. "He's supposed to say, 'Our Father and Mother, who art in heaven,'" he insisted. I quickly realized I had some explaining to do.

Every night before bed, Michael and I say the Lord's Prayer together, and I had taken the liberty of teaching him a more expansive version. How do you explain to a child who has heard all his life that God is both father and mother, that the motherhood of God is not included in this familiar prayer? It wasn't easy, but I did my best.

Saint Paul images God as the midwife who set him apart from his mother's womb, bringing him to birth, calling him through grace to be an apostle. What might happen if you let God be your midwife, bringing to birth new images of God for you to use in your prayer life?

"Therefore I weep with the weeping of Jazer for the vines of Sibmah; I drench you with my tears."... This was the word that the LORD spoke.
Isaiah 16:9, 13

I'd like to visit my mother's grave while I'm in Clarksville," I told Louisa, my oldest and dearest childhood friend. "I could come with you and visit the Judge," she offered, speaking of her father who had been our county's judge.

It was a sultry August afternoon when we visited our parents' graves together. Transfixed and transformed by the moment, we sat at each grave for more than an hour, sharing our memories. We roasted each of our parents and then ourselves—sometimes laughing, sometimes crying, always supporting each other as we sought to understand the meaning of their very different deaths.

There is no doubt in my mind that God was right there beside us, laughing with us, but also crying with us. Several times in Scripture we are told that God mourns with us, suffers with us, and even drenches us with tears. We are never alone in our suffering.

What a gift God gives to us when we need it. Whether we are with a dear, trusted friend or all alone, God is there beside us in our grieving. Can you ask God to be with you in such a time? What would that feel like for you?

When the queen of Sheba heard of the fame of Solomon,....she came to test him with hard questions. She came to Jerusalem...with camels bearing spices, and very much gold, and precious stones; and when she came to Solomon, she told him all that was on her mind.

1 Kings 10:1–2

H ey girl, do I look like the Queen of Sheba, or what?" asked Paula. She strutted into my office wearing a short red dress, big gold earrings, and a fur coat. Her long red nails, complete with gold stars, were glistening. The man of her dreams was in town, and Paula had spared no expense in getting ready.

The Queen of Sheba is best known as a glamorous African queen. However, according to biblical tradition, her appearance is not part of her mystique. Rather, she is portrayed as a ruler of wisdom, wealth, and power. Her abundant self-assurance is obvious. She willingly travels a great distance to test Solomon's wisdom with her own and to speak all that is on her mind.

Here is a woman who does not hold back. When she wants to go, she goes, complete with camels, spices, gold, and precious stones. When she arrives, she doesn't hesitate to meet Solomon as an equal in every way, testing him with hard questions.

What aspects of the Queen of Sheba's character intrigue you most? Why?

Or what woman having ten silver coins, if she loses one of them, does not light a lamp, sweep the house, and search carefully until she finds it? When she has found it, she calls together her friends and neighbors, saying, "Rejoice with me, for I have found the coin that I had lost."

Luke 15:8–9

Many of us are familiar with the image of God as the good shepherd who searches for one lost sheep. In this same passage lies a little-known treasure. Immediately after the good shepherd story, God is described as a woman who diligently sweeps her house in search of one lost coin. What a compelling image of God as a homemaker! How true to life it is.

Have you ever searched tirelessly under furniture for that one, small, lost toy of a child? More than once I have turned over every chair cushion in the house looking for one of my children's prized possessions, whether it was a special toy, a tiny coin, or some other new-found gem. When the search is over, there is always great rejoicing and a sense of completeness. How comforting it is to know that God searches for us with this same intensity until we are safely in the palm of God's hand.

Isn't it amazing that God never ceases to search for us, regardless of how long we may have been lost? Could God be searching for you?

Soon afterwards [Jesus] went on through cities and villages, proclaiming and bringing the good news of the kingdom of God. The twelve were with him, as well as some women who had been cured of evil spirits and infirmities: [one was] Mary, called Magdalene, from whom seven demons had gone out.

Luke 8:1–2

Mary Magdalene is one of the most misunderstood women in Scripture. Although she is often remembered as a prostitute, nowhere in Scripture is this ever mentioned. Rather, we are told that Jesus cures her of seven demons, which most likely refers to depression or epilepsy. She then serves Jesus faithfully throughout his ministry and receives one of the greatest honors in Scripture. According to three of the Gospels, she is the first person to witness the Resurrection.

In Eastern Christian tradition, Mary Magdalene is believed to have journeyed to Rome to tell Caesar about the risen Christ. "To explain this she picked up an egg from the table, whereupon Caesar protested that a human could no more rise from the dead than the egg in her hand could turn red. At once the egg turned blood red, which is why red eggs have been exchanged at Easter for centuries in the Byzantine East. Mary traveled the Mediterranean preaching the Resurrection and died a martyr like Peter and Paul," according to Eastern tradition.[1]

Mary Magdalene is not the only noteworthy woman to be discredited by history. Have you ever been discredited following an achievement? What was that like for you?

1. Sally M. Bucklee, "Oh, to Be in England, Now That Ordination's Here," *Ruach* 15:2 (1994): 8. *Ruach* is the official publication of the Episcopal Women's Caucus.

Joab sent to Tekoa and brought from there a wise woman.... When the woman of Tekoa came to the king, she fell on her face to the ground and did obeisance, and said, "Help, O king!"... Then the woman said, "Please let your servant speak a word to my lord the king." He said, "Speak."

2 Samuel 14:2, 4, 12

B ible stories can be as full of intrigue as a modern day soap opera. The events leading up to the story of the wise woman of Tekoa are a prime example. King David's son Absalom kills his brother, Amnon, because Amnon raped their sister, Tamar. David then expels Absalom from his kingdom. There is no doubt that this is one dysfunctional family.

Joab, one of the king's servants, hopes to secure Absalom's return by soliciting the help of a wise woman. At his suggestion, she dresses as a widow in mourning and tells the king that one of her sons has killed his brother. She then asks the king's advice. He replies, "As the LORD lives, not one hair of your son shall fall to the ground" (v. 11). She then beseeches King David to allow Absalom to return, and her persuasiveness wins the day.

Courage and ingenuity—these are traits we can all use at times. What might you learn from the wise woman of Tekoa?

Since, therefore, [God's] children share flesh and blood, [Jesus] himself like-wise shared the same things.... Therefore he had to become like his brothers and sisters in every respect.

Hebrews 2:14, 17

The fact that Jesus was male has been used historically to deny women the right to ordination. However, the writer of the Letter to the Hebrews makes it clear that as the Christ, or God incarnate, Jesus transcends gender distinctions. Christians believe that Jesus was both human and divine. Through his divinity Jesus becomes "like his brothers and sisters in every respect." Therefore, as women, we are not only made in the image of God, but also in the very image of Christ.

How empowering this can be for us. Why? "Women's imaginations need the deep emotional healing and affirmation that come from seeing the image and likeness of Christ conveyed more fully in relation to them.... To say that Christ cannot be imaged as a woman is to imply that women cannot, in fact, image Christ."[1]

Believing in our hearts that we are made in the image of Christ can have pro-found significance in our lives. How might this knowledge enrich your life?

1. Kathleen Fischer, *Women at the Well* (New York: Paulist Press, 1988), 81.

"Where you go, I will go; where you lodge, I will lodge; your people shall be my people, and your God my God."

Ruth 1:16

Ruth and her mother-in-law, Naomi, enjoy one of the most beautiful friendships in the Bible. They are both widows who need each other's protection to survive in a patriarchal society. Even so, Naomi suggests that Ruth go home to her own family. Ruth then responds with the moving words above.

Ruth and Naomi's relationship is based on mutual dependence and respect. Ruth is a foreigner in an alien land who needs Naomi in order to be accepted, whereas the elderly Naomi needs the protection of Ruth's youth.

They remind me of my friendship with my college roommate, Susan Baker. There is a timelessness to our friendship, borne out of the mutual need of two women in the alien land of college. Like Ruth and Naomi, we relied on each other's strengths to pull us through those important years of transition.

Regardless of how long it's been since Susan and I have seen each other, the years dissolve when we're together. Friendship that withstands the test of time and distance is truly a blessed gift of God. Do you have such a friend in your life? Have you talked to her lately?

But Naomi said to her two daughters-in-law, "Go back each of you to your mother's house."... Then she kissed them, and they wept aloud.... Orpah kissed her mother-in-law, but Ruth clung to her.

Ruth 1:8–9, 14

Orpah is Ruth's sister-in-law. Both women have lost their husbands, as has Naomi before them, and they must all decide what to do with their lives. At first Orpah is determined to follow Ruth and Naomi to live in the foreign land of Judah, but at Naomi's urging Orpah turns back and goes to her own home. We aren't told who is waiting for Orpah, but most likely her family was longing for the day she would return.

Orpah represents most women here. She doesn't lead an army like Deborah, save a life like Miriam, or rule a nation like the Queen of Sheba, but how many of us can make such claims to fame? Precious few. It can be demoralizing to believe that our only role models are superwomen. Women who live their lives believing that relationships and their own homes are important are just as heroic, in their own way, as prophets and great leaders.

It is important for all of us to celebrate not only our public achievements, but our private, everyday ones as well. What do you need to celebrate?

[Jesus said], "Jerusalem, Jerusalem, the city that kills the prophets...who are sent to it! How often have I desired to gather your children together as a hen gathers her brood under her wings, and you were not willing!"
Luke 13:34

Have you ever seen a mother hen, clucking to her chicks, enveloping them with her warmth? She does this to protect the baby chicks from cold and from the danger of hawks or other predators. Jesus wants nothing more for the people of Jerusalem than to lovingly protect them, just as a mother hen protects her brood under her wings.

Jesus' imaging of himself as a mother hen was quoted by both Saint Augustine and Saint Anselm of Canterbury. In the year 1093, Saint Anselm wrote: "But you, Jesus, good lord, are you not also a mother? Are you not that mother who, like a hen, collects her chickens under her wings? Truly, master, you are a mother."[1] Yes, Jesus is our biblical mother also.

What might happen if you prayed to Jesus as your mother?

1. Caroline Walker Bynum, *Jesus as Mother: Studies in the Spirituality of the High Middle Ages* (Berkeley: University of California Press, 1982), 114.

When Jesus saw the crowds,...he began to speak:... "You are the light of the world.... Let your light shine before others, so that they may see your good works and give glory to your Father in heaven."

Matthew 5:1–2, 14, 16

T his Little Light of Mine, I'm Going to Let It Shine." In the words of this simple childhood song lies a great truth, yet one that eludes many people throughout their lives. In my ministry, I've met a number of people who don't believe they have a light to shine. They look around and decide their talents don't measure up, aren't worthy, aren't needed. So they keep their light to themselves, truly believing that they have nothing to give. Yet Jesus tells each one of us, "You are the light of the world." He is not speaking to only some people who have been given special gifts or talents, but to everyone.

What can we do when "this little light of mine" seems shrouded in darkness? First of all, we can remember that the light was never ours to begin with, but God's. Jesus is the light and can become *our* light when we acknowledge the One who dwells within us.

What special light has God given you? What would it take for you to let it shine with such a radiance that everyone could see it?

Paul,... To the church of God that is in Corinth:... I do not want you to be unaware, brothers and sisters, that our ancestors were...baptized into Moses in the cloud and in the sea,...and all drank the same spiritual drink. For they drank from the spiritual rock that followed them, and the rock was Christ.
1 Corinthians 1:1, 2; 10:1–4

How often we forget that the one steadfast presence in our lives is Christ, the Rock upon which all else rests. When we forget, we begin to put our trust in earthly things—people, possessions, jobs. Yet none of these can sustain us in an eternal way. They can even confuse us as we seek to understand who we really are.

In her CD for *The Preacher's Wife*, with great exuberance Whitney Houston sings a spiritual called "I Go to the Rock." The lyrics say it all: "Where do I go when there's nobody else to turn to? Who do I talk to when nobody wants to listen? Who do I lean on when there's no foundation stable? I go to the Rock. I know he's able. I go to the Rock. I'm going to the Rock of my salvation. I'm going to the stone that the builders rejected.... When the earth all around me is sinking sand, on Christ the solid Rock I stand. When I need shelter, when I need a friend, I go to the Rock."[1] Amen.

1. "I Go to the Rock" words and music by Dottie Rambo (copyright 1977 John T. Benson Publishing/ASCAP).

And the one who admits his fault will be kept from failure.
Sirach 20:3

Failure to achieve a desired goal or to repair a broken relationship can be devastating when it happens to us. It's easy to become upset with ourselves, wondering how we could be the cause of our own sadness. Yet such a view doesn't take into account that failing is not always what we think it is.

A friend of mine, who is now the president of a corporation, leads a workshop called, "Fired to Success." It is his contention that people learn far more from their failures than from their successes, if they are willing to look honestly at themselves and their situation. He recounts story after story in which what appeared to be failure actually led to a success that was greater than if everything had gone according to plan.

Failing doesn't mean that we are a failure; it just means we must do things differently next time. Failing doesn't mean we've been disgraced; it just means we dared to try. Failing doesn't mean we're a failure; it just means we have some learning and growing to do. Failing doesn't mean God has abandoned us; it just means we must obediently seek our Lord's will.[1]

What might you learn from your failures?

1. Paraphrased from a poem by an anonymous author.

Now there was a woman who had been suffering from hemorrhages for twelve years. She had endured much under many physicians.... She had heard about Jesus, and came up behind him in the crowd and touched his cloak.... Immediately her hemorrhage stopped.

Mark 5:25–29

One of Gloria Steinem's early essays, "If Men Could Menstruate," still gives me a chuckle. I can't resist sharing it:

So what would happen if suddenly, magically, men could menstruate and women could not? Clearly, menstruation would become an enviable, boast-worthy, masculine event: Young boys would talk about it as the envied beginning of manhood. Gifts, religious ceremonies, family dinners, and stag parties would mark the day.... Doctors would research...everything about cramps.... Only men could serve God and country in combat ("You have to give blood to take blood")...or [as] rabbis ("Without a monthly purge of impurities, women are unclean").... Menopause would be celebrated as a positive event, the symbol that men had accumulated enough years of cyclical wisdom to need no more.[1]

But alas, this was not meant to be.

In Jesus' day, women who were menstruating were considered ritually unclean and therefore untouchable. Even so, Jesus heals a woman who has had an unceasing flow of blood for twelve years. How affirming of womanhood this is. Even so, in some religions today, women are still not allowed to receive communion when they are menstruating.

How might we help our sisters who are treated this way?

1. Gloria Steinem, *Outrageous Acts and Everyday Rebellions* (New York: Holt, Rinehart and Winston, 1983), 338–339.

Thus says the LORD: "We have heard a cry of panic, of terror, and no peace. Ask now, and see, can a man bear a child? Why then do I see every man with his hands on his loins like a woman in labor? Why has every face turned pale?"

Jeremiah 30:5–6

One of my favorite pictures is of Jesus with his head thrown back, having a good laugh. Unfortunately, such portrayals are all too rare. Religion is seen as serious business, with Jesus and God stern-faced and serious, wearing a perpetual air of judgmentalism. Yet these portrayals are contrary to Scripture, where we are told that God weeps, cries, and even makes jokes.

You've never thought of God as a comedian? Well, here it is. I can almost hear the laughter when God teases the men that they look like women in labor, with pale faces and their hands on their loins.

Ethel Barrymore once said, "You grow up the day you have your first real laugh—at yourself." If we can laugh at ourselves and our situations, whatever they may be, our burdens will certainly be lighter. When we forget that God has a sense of humor, perhaps we need to keep this passage close at hand. Our Creator can be a great role model for us here.

Can you share something humorous with God right now?

But Lot's wife, behind him, looked back, and she became a pillar of salt.
Genesis 19:26

One evening, when two angels come to Sodom, Lot urges them to stay in his home. They tell him to leave Sodom immediately with his family because God is about to destroy the town because of the wickedness of the people.

Can you imagine how Lot's wife must have felt when she heard the news? She is suddenly told that she must leave her home and never look back. Regardless of the troubling events in Sodom, it is still her home—the place where she married, lived, and gave birth to her children. In her hasty departure Lot's wife looks back with fondness for one last time, and she becomes a pillar of salt. Nothing is said here about God turning her into a pillar of salt for punishment, as the church has traditionally taught; rather, she *became* a pillar of salt.

Have you ever wept so hard that you felt you might become your tears? Some believe this is what happened to Lot's wife. Can you remember a time in your life when saying good-bye was particularly painful? What might happen if you invited Lot's wife to join you in your memory?

Paul an apostle,...To the churches of Galatia:... There is no longer Jew or Greek, there is no longer slave or free, there is no longer male and female; for all of you are one in Christ Jesus.

Galatians 1:1–2; 3:28

S aint Paul states clearly here that we are all the same in the eyes of God. Slave and free, male and female, we are all one in Christ Jesus. As part of the body of Christ we are all equal, yet distinctly different parts. Since this is so clearly stated, it's hard to understand why the Christian world still operates on a patri-archal model.

In *Reviving Ophelia: Saving the Selves of Adolescent Girls*, Mary Pipher describes our culture as not only patriarchal, but also girl-poisoning. She writes, "[Adolescent girls] lose their assertive, energetic, and 'tomboyish' personalities and become more deferential, self-critical and depressed." She goes on to state that adolescent girls are pressured by the culture to be persons they are not, a culture that is rife with girl-hurting "isms," particularly sexism.[1] Unfortunately, the Christian church has become part of the culture in this regard, rather than standing against it for a healthier society.

We owe it to our daughters to right this wrong. How might you help?

1. Mary Pipher, *Reviving Ophelia: Saving the Selves of Adolescent Girls* (New York: Ballantine Books, 1994) 19, 230.

While [Pilate] was sitting on the judgment seat, his wife sent word to him, "Have nothing to do with that innocent man, for today I have suffered a great deal because of a dream about him."

Matthew 27:19

During Jesus' trial, only one person speaks out on his behalf, the wife of Pontius Pilate. Since Pilate is the only one with the authority to condemn Jesus to death, her intercession could have saved his life.

I wonder how she must have felt. A woman in her culture had no standing in the law. She was considered to be the property of her husband, who was most certainly not accustomed to taking advice from her. Yet she willingly risks her relationship with her husband and her own reputation to stand up for Jesus.

Who overrides her pleas for Jesus' innocence? The chief priests and the elders, who persuade the crowds to have Jesus killed. It is only after they become involved that the crowd shouts, "Let him be crucified!" (v. 23).

So this one lone woman is right, while all the chief priests and elders are wrong. Imagine how she must have felt. Acting on her own intuition, she tries to tell everyone that the whole proceeding is evil, but her words go unheeded.

Have you ever had a similar experience? How did you feel?

[Jesus] called the crowd with his disciples, and said to them, "If any want to become my followers, let them deny themselves and take up their cross and follow me."

Mark 8:34

H ave you ever poured out your soul to someone and been told, "Don't worry; everything's going to be all right. That's just your cross to bear"? At one point in my life I thought that the more crosses I was carrying, the better Christian I was. Not only could I suffer and carry my own cross, but give me half a chance and I would gladly carry yours as well. I should have had a card printed that said "Professional Cross Carrier—No Load Too Heavy," or in today's vernacular, "Codependent at Large."

Codependency is nothing more than carrying someone else's cross for them. Somewhere, for some of us, the message became distorted. Taking up our cross and following Jesus became confused. We forgot that what Jesus said is, "Take up *your* cross." Not someone else's, just yours and yours alone. He also said, "Take up your cross," not "your cross*es*." One cross. So it's yours and there is only one. What freedom can come with this realization!

Are you carrying someone else's cross for them? Why?

From noon on, darkness came over the whole land until three in the after-noon.... Then Jesus cried again with a loud voice and breathed his last.
                                                        Matthew 27:45, 50

The agony of Christ on the cross is the agony of the birth pangs of a new creation. Just as God gives birth to creation and endures the pains of labor on our behalf, so too does Jesus when he gives birth to the new creation on the cross. Through the Crucifixion, Jesus experiences something not unlike the desperate pain of a mother dying in childbirth.

Christ giving birth to the church on the cross is vividly depicted in a thirteenth-century French Bible. In an illumination, the church is depicted as a baby being born out of Christ's side. How it startled me when I first saw this illumination! Just above this image was a depiction of Eve being born out of the side of Adam, from his rib. This image was more familiar to me. Then I slowly began to see the connection. Saint Paul describes Jesus as the new Adam, ushering in a new creation. Both Adams, in a sense, give birth.

How might our lives be different if we could believe that Christ gave birth on the cross to new life for us?

And when they had crucified [Jesus],...many women were also there, looking on from a distance; they had followed Jesus from Galilee and had provided for him. Among them were Mary Magdalene, and Mary the mother of James and Joseph, and the mother of the sons of Zebedee.

Matthew 27:35, 55–56

While the apostles flee from Jesus' crucifixion in fear, the women steadfastly remain, never leaving their Savior alone during his darkest hour. The most wonderful passage I've ever read about the faithfulness of these women is in *Are Women Human?* by Dorothy L. Sayers. She writes:

Perhaps it is no wonder that the women were first at the Cradle and last at the Cross. They had never known a man like this Man—there never has been such another. A prophet and teacher who never nagged at them, never flattered or coaxed or patronized; who never made arch jokes about them, never treated them either as "The women, God help us!" or "The ladies, God bless them!"; who rebuked without querulousness and praised without condescension; who took their questions and arguments seriously, who never mapped out their sphere for them.... There is no act, no sermon, no parable in the whole Gospel that borrows its pungency from female perversity; nobody could possibly guess from the words and deeds of Jesus that there was anything "funny" about woman's nature.[1]

What a gift Jesus has given to all women! Can you thank him for this blessing?

1. Dorothy L. Sayers, *Are Women Human?* (Grand Rapids, Mich.: William B. Eerdman's Publishing, 1971), 47.

But on the first day of the week, at early dawn, [the women] came to the tomb…. They found the stone rolled away from the tomb, but when they went in, they did not find the body. While they were perplexed about this, suddenly two men in dazzling clothes stood beside them.

Luke 24:1–4

I n the midst of their heartbreak, utter dejection, and defeat, expecting nothing but a lifeless form, the women rise early and go to the tomb. Even though they are perplexed and terrified, they nevertheless walk straight into the empty tomb. They walk into darkness and find light. They walk into emptiness and find fullness. They walk in alone and find angels there to guide them.

To find new life, we too must walk into the empty tomb in our lives. We must walk into that place where we most fear being. How we avoid these dark corners of our lives! Yet, only when we have the courage to walk in will they no longer hold power over our lives. Only when we walk into the tomb, which is womblike, can we experience new life, rebirth.

Where is the empty tomb in your life? What is it that lies before you, gaping in blackness and uncertainty? Can you, like these women, have the courage to walk in?

Paul,... To the church of God that is in Corinth:... And so, brothers and sisters, I could not speak to you as spiritual people, but rather as people of the flesh, as infants in Christ. I fed you with milk, not solid food.

1 Corinthians 1:1, 2; 3:1–2

Y ou know, Elizabeth," said Frank, "the best mother I ever had was a man." His words startled me because the idea of a male mother was unthinkable to me. "What do you mean?" I blurted out. "I don't understand."

Frank's mother had died in a car accident when he was seven years old, leaving a void in his life that seemed impossible to fill. Many years later, while on a spiritual retreat, he met a monk—a loving, caring man who nurtured him and cared for him as a mother cares for her children. Over time he realized that God had sent the monk into his life to fill the void left by his mother's untimely death; the healing balm of that relationship continues to bear fruit in Frank's life today.

In biblical times, only the mother fed an infant with milk. Here, Saint Paul once again uses the image of a mother to describe himself, joyfully uplifting the feminine. Could it be that Saint Paul is also our biblical mother?

Who are the special people in your life who have mothered you?

*But Mary [Magdalene] stood weeping outside the tomb.... Jesus said to her,...
"Go to my brothers and say to them, 'I am ascending to my Father and your
Father, to my God and your God.' " Mary Magdalene went and announced to
the disciples, "I have seen the Lord"; and she told them that he had said these
things to her.*

John 20:11, 17–18

Three of the four Gospels record Jesus' first resurrection appearance as having been to Mary Magdalene. Is it significant that this event, which lies at the center of the Christian faith, is recorded as having been revealed first of all to a woman? Not only does Mary Magdalene first see the risen Christ, but Jesus sends her forth to proclaim the good news to the apostles, prompting Saint Bernard of Clairvaux, in the thirteenth century, to refer to her as an "apostle to the apostles." Her role was so significant that she was canonized as a saint.

I once saw a cartoon in which the risen Christ is commissioning Mary Magdalene to witness to the eleven apostles. As he does so, a voice from heaven thunders, "But don't think this means you can be ordained or anything!" Since a woman is the first person in Scripture commissioned by Jesus to tell the good news of the resurrection, it's hard to understand why women are still denied ordination in some religious traditions today.

Why do you suppose Jesus chose to appear first to Mary Magdalene, rather than to one of his eleven apostles? Is there a message here for women today? For the church?

Let us consider how to provoke one another to love and good deeds, not neglecting to meet together,...but encouraging one another.
Hebrews 10:24–25

S oon after the birth of our first child, Charlotte, I joined a "baby group" with three other first-time mothers. What encouragement we offered to one another in our unfamiliar, baffling roles as new mothers. "Will my baby ever sleep through the night?" was an often-asked question, as we wondered aloud how anyone survives the rigors of motherhood.

As time went on we decided that we should no longer intervene in our children's squabbles. Never mind that they were only two years old. Within a short time, they were all on the floor, tackling each other and pulling each other's hair out. We soon realized that perhaps our timing was a bit off.

We wondered. Could we be the mothers that our children needed in today's world? The terrible twos couldn't hold a candle to the worry of adolescence, and we knew it. Were we up to the task?

With extended family far away, groups of women meeting together for support and encouragement are a much needed lifeline in today's world. Who are the people who support you? Have you seen them lately?

Now in Joppa there was a disciple whose name was Tabitha, which in Greek is Dorcas. She was devoted to good works and acts of charity. At that time she became ill and died.... [Peter] turned to the body and said, "Tabitha, get up." Then she opened her eyes, and seeing Peter, she sat up.... This became known throughout Joppa, and many believed in the Lord.

Acts 9:36–42

A woman named Dorcas, who is identified as a disciple, is the only person in Scripture to be raised from the dead by an apostle. Yet, how many of us have ever heard of this miraculous act of Peter? Imagine the response when he simply says, "Get up," and she sits up!

Who is this special, though little-known, woman? Dorcas is a seamstress who sews beautiful garments for the people of her village. In addition, she is known for her acts of charity. When news of Dorcas's being raised from the dead spreads throughout the country, many people begin to believe in Christ. Once again, the witness of a woman, whether by her words or actions, has a powerful effect.

Our words and actions can have a similar effect today. There's a song, "And they'll know we are Christians by our love, by our love, and they'll know we are Christians by our love." What do people know about you by your actions?

Paul,... To the church of God that is in Corinth:... For we are the temple of the living God.

2 Corinthians 1:1; 6:16

God means for us to treat our bodies gently, with love, to exercise regularly, and even to pamper ourselves occasionally with a manicure or a massage. It sounds simple, but it really isn't. Being God's temple is a tall order, and handling it properly can require a difficult balancing act. While we are to love and reverence our bodies, we are not meant to worship them. Cosmetics are a $20-billion-a-year industry worldwide. The amount spent on cosmetics in a year could buy 400,000 four-year university scholarships for women, or fund 2,000 women's health clinics or 33,000 battered-women's shelters.[1] In addition, the cosmetic surgery industry in the United States grosses more than $300 million each year.[2] Taking care of our bodies is one thing, being obsessed with how we look is another.

Now, don't get me wrong; I'm the first to wear makeup. I decided some time ago that if I'm created in God's image, surely God would delight in that image looking as good as possible. But there are limits. Again, moderation and balance are the keys.

Do you have a healthy balance in your life in this regard? If not, what might you do differently?

1. Naomi Wolf, *The Beauty Myth* (New York: William Morrow, 1991), 113.
2. Standard & Poor's Industry Surveys, 1988, quoted in Wolf, *The Beauty Myth*, 232.

Perfect love casts out fear.

1 John 4:18

In her book, *A Return to Love*, Marianne Williamson writes poignantly about an aspect of fear not usually discussed. We often tend to focus on our fear of failure, but perhaps this is only part of the picture. She writes:

Our deepest fear is not that we are inadequate.
Our deepest fear is that we are powerful beyond measure.
It is our light, not our darkness that most frightens us.
We ask ourselves, who am I to be brilliant, gorgeous, talented, and fabulous?
Actually, who are you not to be?
You are a child of God. Your playing small doesn't serve the world.
There's nothing enlightened about shrinking so that other people won't feel insecure around you.
We were born to make manifest the glory of God that is within us.
It's not just in some of us; it's in everyone.
And as we let our own light shine, we unconsciously give other people permission to do the same.
As we are liberated from our own fears, our presence automatically liberates others.[1]

Do you see yourself anywhere in Williamson's words? How would it feel to accept that you are "powerful beyond measure"?

1. Marianne Williamson, *A Return to Love* (New York: HarperCollins, 1992), 165.

But now thus says the LORD,... "You are precious in my sight."
                                            Isaiah 43:1, 4

As I write this meditation, I am flying home from the funeral of Diana, Princess of Wales. No, I didn't receive an invitation; I was in the crowd outside Westminster Abbey where, several commentators said, the real funeral took place. We sang hymns and responded to prayers, as people silently cried.

As Earl Spencer gave his moving tribute to his sister Diana, my heart stood still when he said, "For all the status, the glamour, the applause, Diana remained throughout a very insecure person at heart, almost childlike in her desire to do good for others so she could release herself from deep feelings of unworthiness." Thousands of bouquets of flowers, each with a loving note, had been tearfully placed in her honor. Several billion people watched her funeral. Yet, in her lifetime, Diana did not feel loved.

Aren't most of us, too, loved far more than we realize, not only by our loved ones, but by God? Every person on earth is precious in God's sight.

When God has spoken so clearly, why do we, like Diana, sometimes listen to messages that tell us otherwise?

Paul,... To all God's beloved in Rome:...Greet Andronicus and Junia, my relatives who were in prison with me; they are prominent among the apostles, and they were in Christ before I was.

Romans 1:1, 7; 16:7

A woman named as an apostle in Scripture? Surely this is banner news to be publicized wherever Christianity is taught or preached. Each child in Sunday school should know about the twelve apostles named by Jesus and the other two named by Saint Paul. Fourteen apostles? There can't be! Surely we would have heard of it by now.

Junia, a woman, and Andronicus, a man, are indeed named by Saint Paul as apostles, who are imprisoned along with him for their beliefs. Nowhere else in Scripture does Saint Paul name anyone as an apostle other than himself and the original twelve. Yet here he names both Junia and Andronicus not only as apostles, but as prominent among them. The strength of their convictions is borne out by their willingness to go to prison for their beliefs. It is believed that perhaps they were a husband and wife ministry team.

What does it mean that Saint Paul named a woman as an apostle in the first century? Does this bear any relevance for the role of women in the church today? What could it mean in your life?

The next day we left and came to Caesarea; and we went into the house of Philip the evangelist.... He had four unmarried daughters who had the gift of prophecy.

Acts 21:8–9

I 've got the perfect title for your new book, *Women on Top: A Guide to Fulfillment,*" exclaimed my husband, Michael. We were sitting at a cigar bar. Never mind that I could barely breathe. I've discovered that when one is married to a cigar enthusiast, it's a great place for conversation and well worth the drawbacks.

"That's not what my book's about," I said. "It's not about women or men on top. It's about mutually supportive partners working together."

I hope I've communicated that as women, we're meant to feel good about ourselves in a healthy way. We are not meant to use our sense of self-worth to denigrate anyone, male or female, but rather to live more fully into all that God created us to be. In addition, I hope I've provided you with models of women who were able to do that more than 2,000 years ago, like Philip's four daughters, who are designated as prophets.

If these women can live into God's will for them in their culture, I know we can do so in ours. What steps might you take to do so?

The Lord is my rock, my fortress, and my deliverer, my God, my rock, in whom I take refuge.

Psalm 18:2

Will you assist at my wedding?" my father asked me. For more than a year he had been dating Mary Nell, a delightful widow he had met at church. She was the answer to our family's prayers. Even so, I was concerned about the emotions I would feel during their marriage service.

Before agreeing, I decided to visit the church. I stood quietly in front of the altar as memories flooded over me. I was standing in the very spot where I had been baptized, confirmed, and married, and where my mother's coffin had rested. Could I now stand there, as a priest, and assist at my father's wedding?

That afternoon I realized that the altar represented God as a Rock to me. Years had come and gone, the carpet surrounding it had been changed twice, but the altar was still there, through times of unspeakable joy and unbearable sorrow. I realized, then, how blessed I was to have such continuity in my life, and I knew that God would be with me yet again.

"I now pronounce you husband and wife," I proudly beamed.

Some stories still have happy endings.

BENEDICTION

Yes, some stories still do have happy endings, and sometimes we are blessed with several. Shortly after completing this book, I was deeply in prayer, when suddenly I felt my mother's presence in a profound way. I sensed a gentleness of spirit about her, a peace, which I had never experienced in her presence.

"I'm healed, Betsy," I felt her saying to me. "I'm healed, now." "I'm so happy for you," was all I could think, as my whole being filled with unimaginable joy. I felt as if a mantle of pure love being placed around my shoulders. I then realized that, in part, this book has been about my own healing. With the deepest gratitude I have ever felt, I thanked God for blessing me with this most precious of gifts.

And now I must thank you for joining me on this journey. My fervent prayer is that through the words of this book, someone, even one person, will begin to feel a gentleness of spirit, a peace, which has previously eluded them.

Yes, "My soul is satisfied as with a rich feast, and my mouth praises you with joyful lips" (Psalm 63:5). Thanks be to God, our comforting mother, rock, midwife—our mother bear. Amen. Allelulia.

Praise for *Entertaining Angels:*
Hospitality Programs for the Caring Church
also by Elizabeth Rankin Geitz

"I have an extensive collection of books in the areas of church growth, evangelism, and newcomer ministry. I have placed *Entertaining Angels* in the section reserved for the very best. It should be mandatory reading for those in evangelism and hospitality ministries."

> *The Reverend George Martin*
> *Director, Church Ad Project*

"[Mainline churches] might learn to do better with people who have had the courage to find their way across a sanctuary threshold, often to be turned off by the indifference and apathetic inside. Geitz would quicken their interest, open doors."
> *Christian Century*

"...a buoyant book about our ministry as guests and hosts...an eminently practical guide to the mysterious art of welcoming strangers to the glory of God."
> *The Reverend Dr. John T. Koenig, author of* New Testament
> Hospitality *and* Rediscovering New Testament Prayer

Praise for *Gender and the Nicene Creed*
also by Elizabeth Rankin Geitz

"It is to be hoped that Elizabeth Rankin Geitz will be heard. Her *Gender and the Nicene Creed* is a small book, but it proposes a large change. Believing that 'tradition is a living tradition,' Geitz seeks to recover and recapture lost feminine traditions of the church through 'sound biblical, historical, and theological principles.' ... 'digging below the surface of commonly held understandings,' Geitz discovers how the Creed reveals the feminine attributes of God and the feminine traditions of Christianity."

Publishers Weekly Religion BookLine

"...a serious and penetrating reflection, practical and popular but at the same time academically responsible...solid research and careful reasoning....This book...helps people to understand what are the underlying issues in the contemporary debate over inclusive language....it is even more helpful for this purpose than the study materials that have so far been provided by those who are officially charged with this process."

Anglican Theological Review